*Through the
Fish's Eye*

An Outdoor Life Book

Through the Fish's Eye

An Angler's Guide to Gamefish Behavior

Mark Sosin
John Clark

drawings by Dorothea Barlowe

Outdoor Life

Harper & Row
New York, Evanston, San Francisco, London

Published by Book Division, Times Mirror Magazines, Inc.

Third Printing, 1978

Library of Congress Catalog Card Number: 72-97172

ISBN:

Contents

1

Know
Your
Quarry

No matter how sophisticated an angler you may be, fishing will always have an element of mystery. If the mystery and the challenge weren't there, fishing would not be a sport. Favored gamefishes are those that provide a real but predictable challenge. In reverse, the game is one of defense in which the fish must avoid being caught. Nature takes care of this by genetic adaptation: the smartest fish survive to spawn and thus give birth to even smarter fish; the vulnerable are caught, and the weak strains are eliminated.

The overall effect is actually to build up a strain of fish that is resistant to capture. As the fish learn to avoid each new method, angling becomes more difficult. New techniques must be devised to replace those used by anglers in the past. Of necessity, these must be born from a thorough understanding of the habits and characteristics of the species sought.

The emphasis in this book is on *why* fish react the way they do and *why* certain fishing methods produce better results than others. We hope that when you finish this book, you'll have a better idea of why fish behave the way they do. We have relied on scientific facts based on research by qualified men and women who have devoted their lives to the study of fish.

If you can anticipate how a fish will react under a given set of circumstances, you should be able to come up with the correct method of catching that fish. How well you do really depends on how determined you are in applying yourself to the task at hand. You might enjoy yourself by merely sitting alongside a pond and letting a bait dangle beneath the surface; or you may take your fishing seriously and wish to improve. How fast you progress is up to you.

If there is a secret to fishing, it rests with your own powers of observation. We hope to stimulate some new ideas, but you're the one who will have to evaluate each individual situation. Once you decide what is taking place, you should be able to apply some of the principles that have been established. We can only describe what motivates your quarry as well as offering suggestions on how to handle the situation.

About 70 percent of the earth's surface is covered with water and almost all of that water supports some type of aquatic life. Fish are found at altitudes of over 15,000 feet and at depths of almost 35,000 feet. Most of the species with which we are concerned as sport fishermen inhabit inland waters and the coastal environment inside the continental shelf. Scientists, by the way, estimate that there are between 15,000 and 17,000 species of fish on earth today, compared to about 8,600 birds and 4,500 mammals.

Each fish plays a unique role in nature. Every species has its own life and its own strategy for survival. The brook trout and brown trout may look very much alike, but they remain as separate species because there are pronounced differences in their strategies and life cycles. The tunas are high-speed predators roaming the oceans and running down their prey with tremendous bursts of energy. To succeed in this role, their bodies have the perfect fusiform shape, and the muscle structure going to the tail is massive. The large-mouth bass, on the other hand, comes close to the perfect all-round predator and its shape advertises this fact. The bass is not built for long bursts of speed, but its wide, sweeping tail enables it to launch an attack quickly and effectively.

HOW A FISH IS BUILT

Understanding how a fish is built is the first step in improving your angling skills. We know that a fish lives in a medium of water—a fluid—that serves as its home, grocery store, playground, and even its grave. So the average fish must suit the special conditions and circumstances of underwater life.

A fish, like any other vertebrate, must be able to find and ingest food for energy. It must have a system of locomotion particularly suited to life in a fluid. Oxygen must enter the system to burn the fuel (food), and there must be a method of protection against enemies and damaging natural forces. Finally, our fish must be able to reproduce itself and have control over all bodily systems.

The basic make-up of all animals includes a frame, a mouth and digestive system, a respiratory and circulatory system, a sensory and nervous system, organs for internal functioning, and an outer covering. A fish possesses all these attributes, but it must make them work underwater.

Knowing this, let's look at a typical fish. We start with the frame, which provides support for all the components and determines the shape, which is streamlined and pointed at the front to enable the fish to move easily through the water. A bony case protects the delicate brain and leaves openings for the eyes, nostrils, glands, mouth, and gills.

Additional framework supports the rest of the body and houses the internal organs. It is flexible but strong. The backbone is the central member of this frame. It attaches to the skull on one end and to the tail on the other. It is made of small segments of bone (vertebrae), joined together with flexible couplings called cartilage. Its hollow center contains the delicate central nerve cord.

ANATOMY OF A FISH

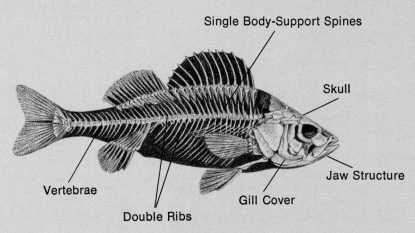

Single Body-Support Spines

Skull

Jaw Structure

Gill Cover

Double Ribs

Vertebrae

SKELETON

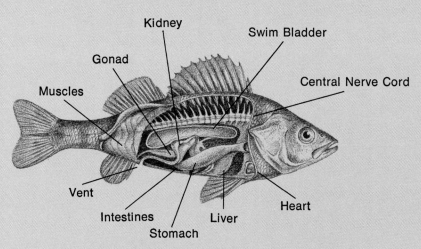

Kidney

Swim Bladder

Gonad

Central Nerve Cord

Muscles

Heart

Vent

Liver

Intestines

Stomach

MUSCLES AND INTERNAL ORGANS

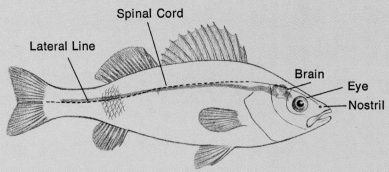

Spinal Cord

Lateral Line

Brain

Eye

Nostril

NERVOUS AND SENSORY SYSTEMS

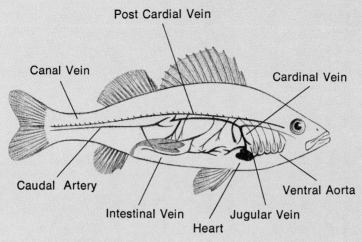

Post Cardial Vein

Canal Vein

Cardinal Vein

Caudal Artery

Ventral Aorta

Intestinal Vein

Jugular Vein

Heart

CIRCULATORY FEATURES

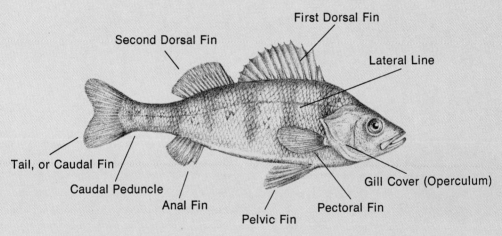

First Dorsal Fin

Second Dorsal Fin

Lateral Line

Tail, or Caudal Fin

Caudal Peduncle

Anal Fin

Gill Cover (Operculum)

Pelvic Fin

Pectoral Fin

EXTERNAL FEATURES

Spines in each vertebral segment, running upward and downward, support the muscles. Since the internal organs are below the backbone, the lower spines double to form ribs for strength and protection. Propulsion comes from the tail, the main power tool, which has a bony framework for strength. A main jawbone and supplementary jawbones ensure that the mouth can open wide and close swiftly. Covering plates that are thin, tough, and flexible encase the gills.

A guidance system is necessary for maneuverability under-

water. One or more dorsal fins on top and an anal fin underneath act as anti-roll stabilizers. Two pairs of fins—one at the
shoulder and one underneath the body—with the necessary
attaching bones, give the fish maneuverability. A single pair
would not allow for quick tilting of the body. All of the fins
require numerous thin supports for maximum suppleness and
strength. These supports extend into the muscle and meet or
overlap with the spinal column spines.

Muscle masses provide power and give the fish a streamlined shape for efficient movement in water. The fastest fish
have their greatest girth one-third of the way back from the
snout. Tests have shown that this is the perfect hydrodynamic shape. In order to develop speed underwater, a fish
must undulate its body in waves, creating a ripple effect
along the muscles. The main muscles are attached in segments so that each can be triggered to fire in series from head
to tail. The strongest contractions occur near the tail to create
the snap that provides the main thrust. Supplementary
muscles activate the jaw, fins, gill covers, heart, eyes, and
head.

The sensory system starts with the eyes, one on either side
of the head, placed well forward to provide all-around vision
with some binocular vision in a cone ahead of the fish. Eye-
lids are not necessary because the eyes are immersed constantly in water. And distant vision is not provided because
the natural turbidity of water prevents fish, under most circumstances, from seeing very far. An adjustment mechanism
enables the fish to see both at night and during the daytime.
There is a good system for color perception in most species.

The fish also has an olfactory system. It relies on smell for
feeding at night, sensing at a distance (because vision is limited), and for bottom feeding in muddy water. Migratory
fish, especially, often have a supersensitive sense of smell to
home in on locations.

A fish is able to taste-test its food even before it puts the
food in its mouth. Taste sensors on fins and barbels accomplish this, together with some taste buds in the mouth. Fish
that root in the mud find this system extremely useful. At the
same time, a system of touch helps our fish reject inedible

objects (like hooks or lures), and is useful for orientation, for schooling, and for sex. An extremely sensitive temperature sensing system enables the fish to distinguish temperature changes within a fraction of one degree.

Next, the fish needs an auditory system so it can hear. Sound carries much better underwater than it does in air, and since the fish is immersed in water, it doesn't need the same auditory equipment as mammals. Instead, the ears are *inside* the head, the eardrum eliminated. Sound is transmitted from the water through the bone in the fish's head to the ear. Neither does the fish need outer earflaps, which would only get in the way and slow its swimming speed. Because of limited visibility and the preferences of some species for night feeding, hearing is extremely important. Our fish can hear its enemies approaching, detect water movements, and even respond to the flutterings of a wounded baitfish. In addition, the fish possesses a lateral line along each side of the body near the middle that stretches from the head to the tail. This lateral line is sensitive to vibrations and permits the fish to "hear" low-frequency sounds coming from every direction.

All these systems are tied together by a network of nerves. The nerves carry messages back and forth to signal muscles and sensing systems into action. The message center is the brain, and it has several compartments. Vision and smell require much larger compartments, but the entire structure is not very large in relation to the whole fish because most of its reactions are instinctive rather than learned.

A balancing organ composed of two cavities, filled with fluid and nerve endings, contains an earstone to trigger the specific nerves to provide different angles of attitude. A swim bladder—similar to a balloon filled with gas—helps the fish to conserve energy and to benefit from the heavier medium of water by giving it a neutral weight.

A circulatory system connects all of the organs. An outgoing system (arteries) carries food to the cells as well as oxygen, while the return system (veins) brings back wastes and carbon dioxide. Tiny capillaries form a bridge across each cell to make the system work effectively.

The heart acts as a pump to push blood through the circulatory system. It is located close to the gills where oxygen is filtered out of the water through tiny filaments of delicate membrane.

If our fish is going to grow and survive, it needs a mouth to ingest food, and teeth to prevent prey from escaping. A tongue helps the fish to manipulate its prey. Gill rakers on the inside of the gills help to strain smaller foods out of the water. The mouth opening is connected through a tube to the stomach and the small and large intestines.

An opening at the end of the intestines provides for the disposal of solid wastes. Gasses filter out of the gills and into the water. A kidney organ filters liquid wastes from the blood, which are passed through a duct and into the water.

If our fish is to reproduce itself, it needs a reproductive system—one to make eggs (in the female) and another to make sperm (in the male)—with a storage chamber for ripe products and a duct leading to the outside.

Finally, the outer covering (skin) controls the passage of fluids in and out of the body and covers and ties in the various systems. The skin is protected by a covering of scales. Protective coloration helps the fish to feed effectively and conceals it from its enemies. The skin is darker on the top and lighter on the bottom, the colors blending in the mid-section.

The angler's goal is to catch this fish.

2

Swimming

Fish are equipped with refined propulsion systems. For both defense and for hunting down prey, each fish species has its own specialized form of locomotion. Sensing danger, a tuna will use its fine propulsion system to move swiftly to a safer place, while the largemouth bass with its versatile fin structure and flat tail will probably maneuver itself beneath a log or similar cover.

To understand the moves fish make and why they make them requires knowledge of how shape determines natural havens; why the fin structure may be crucial to one species and unnecessary in another, or simply why speed is important to some species and not to others.

If you know how a fish is built, you have a good indication of how it is going to react when hooked, even if you have never fought that type of fish before. By knowing what to expect from a fish, and anticipating its moves, you stand a better chance of landing it. Simply understanding the propulsion system of fish, gives you an insight into how they feed and survive. When the propulsion system of a fish is not geared for high-speed swimming, it will seldom chase a lure moving at top speed. Likewise, a species that encounters difficulty in maneuvering or turning sharply may miss an erratic lure and never try a second attack if it fails on the first pass.

HOW FISH SWIM

Fish swim by undulating their bodies in a snakelike motion. The undulations pass down the fish's body in muscle waves and each wave ends in a snap of the tail. Forward thrust comes from the backward push against water created by muscle wave, tail snap, or both.

Long, thin fish such as walleyes rely more on muscle wave and less on tail snap. Short, stocky fish such as largemouth bass cannot undulate their bodies so well and therefore depend more on their tails. That's why the largemouth's tail is larger in proportion to its body than is a walleye's. Thinner fish gain by being more pliable and able to bend themselves from side to side, producing undulations. They lose, however, by having less muscle along their sides with which to impart truly powerful thrusts to their tails.

A thin fish, such as a pike or barracuda, doesn't offer much resistance to the water and therefore the escape technique of turning broadside when hooked doesn't work as well. Its torpedo-shaped body is designed to cut through the water and, even when it is broadside, it is relatively easy to turn its head by rod pressure.

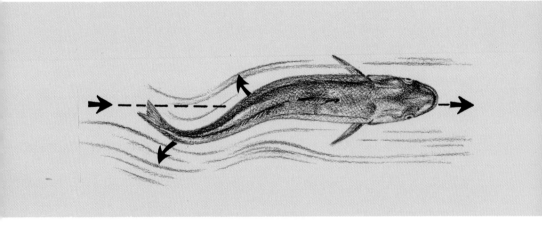

Fish swim by undulating their bodies in a snakelike motion and snapping their tails. The push of the muscle waves and the beat of the tail against the water (arrows) produce forward thrust.

Most of a fish's muscle is used for swimming, including all the flesh from the head to the tail. On close inspection, you can see that the muscle layer is made of dozens of segments, or flakes. Each segment is controlled separately, and in swimming, the muscle waves pass along the fish in a ripple effect as the contraction of one segment after another is triggered automatically. When one segment on the right side is in full contraction, its opposite on the left side is in full expansion. As each succeeding wave reaches the tail section, many segments contract simultaneously to pull the tail fin strongly to the side. This produces the strong thrust of the tail.

The basic form of fish tail is a flat blade made up of thin rods of bone with a membrane stretched over them like a Japanese fan. The tail is attached firmly to the end of the spine by bony plates, ligaments, and muscles that provide strength but allow for great suppleness. A soft, pliant tail of large size gives the greatest efficiency for quick powerful starts and for the maximum amount of power at a relatively slow rate of tail beat.

The largemouth bass typifies fish in this category. In approaching a lure or bait underwater, a bass will glide toward it slowly with a few slow beats of the tail. The strike, particularly on the surface, is an explosion as a few sweeps of the broad tail catapaults the bass toward the bait. That same powerful tail will drive a hooked bass for the nearest lily pads or weedbed, and if you manage to stop the fish, you can actually feel the slow but immensely strong tail beat. In open water, the runs are short, because the bass is not designed for long, sustained runs. Instead, it relies on power rather than maneuverability to win its freedom.

The trout's tail is about one-sixth of the fish's length and twice as wide at the end as it is at the base, when normally expanded. With a rearward edge nearly straight from corner to corner, the tail is thin enough to provide maximum suppleness and minimum drag, yet strong enough to stand the abuse of digging a nest in the gravel for its eggs. The tail provides power for a top cruising speed of about 5 miles per hour in strong currents, and for the thrust and maneuverabil-

Lurking among the coral sea fans on the ocean floor, a great barracuda sights a quarry *(above)*. With a beat of its tail, the fish darts
forward *(below)*, then cleaves the water at full speed by the powerful undulations of its long body *(right)*.

ity needed to develop sudden bursts of speed up to 10 miles per hour to capture prey or escape predators. A trout moves approximately one-half of its body length for each snap of the tail. Not relying upon high-speed pursuits to capture its prey, a trout, instead, lies in wait, and with a quick thrust of its tail grabs a mayfly or a minnow in an instant.

In contrast, the tail of the tuna is highly developed and specialized for sustained speed, making tuna among the fastest of all fishes. The leading edges, both top and bottom, are thick, hard, and fixed in position. The center is strongly forked. The tuna tail, which appears small for the size of the fish and the power it delivers, functions in a special way. Whereas, most species swing the tail from side to side as a result of body undulations, the tuna beats its tail violently in a short arc 10 or 20 times per *second*. One tail beat drives the tuna about one length of its body. To swim at 20 miles per hour, a 30-inch tuna must make about 17 tail beats per second. In the tradeoff, however, tuna end up with very poor maneuverability. They can chase down any form of prey in open pursuit on a straight run, but turning quickly is another matter. When driving bait down to the bottom, they often smack into the sand simply because they can't stop or turn. Slower but highly mobile prey can escape a tuna more easily than can faster, less maneuverable species.

Fishing for tuna can take on a new dimension for the angler who understands these facts about his opponent. A tuna can easily run down a trolled bait or lure regardless of boat speed. Knowing this, skippers often drag baits at a fast pace so they can cover more ocean in the same period of time. But the truly significant point is the tuna's lack of maneuverability. A feather or cedar plug that moves through the water with a minimum of lateral movement is a far better choice of lures than a bait that will dart and dive. If the tuna miscalculates a sudden movement, it will miss the lure completely.

Squid forms a basic part of the tuna's diet in some waters, along with mackerel and other bait fish that swim relatively straight. We once observed the tuna's unique propulsion system in action over Bermuda's Challenger Banks. The cap-

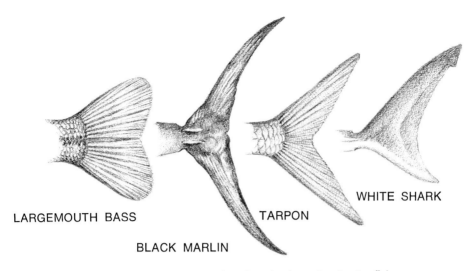

LARGEMOUTH BASS

TARPON

BLACK MARLIN

WHITE SHARK

Four types of tail shapes found on fresh- and saltwater fishes.

tain threw handfuls of dead anchovies and hog-mouthed fry in the water and the Allison tuna boiled on the surface in a feeding rampage. We saw immediately that the tuna could not manuever in the chum, but instead set a course straight through it, swallowing a piece or two in their path, and then made a wide turn to come back through it again.

The special features of body structure that typify a species of fish also indicate something about its style of swimming and how it will react. The pikes, characterized by long, thin bodies with sharp snouts, are well designed for fast pursuit in open water. Because of their large dorsal and anal fins, set well back toward their tails, they have unusual takeoff power for lightening-quick strikes at their prey. But they have sacrificed maneuverability for speed. Once on a lunge, pike cannot change course easily, and this gives the more agile baitfish a chance to escape if they dart to the side just as the pike starts its strike. For this reason, it is more difficult for a member of the pike family to hit a darting-type plug or lure. As a general rule, when a fish lacks maneuverability, artificial lures should be of the type that follow a relatively straight path. That's why the wobbling spoon is more successful than the darters. The flashy finish will attract the pike and once he zeros in, the spoon won't deviate from his path of attack.

Because of the straight strike, pike are experts at guerilla warfare, driving hard to attack from short range. Like snakes,

Long, thin-bodied pike is perfectly suited to fast pursuit in open water. Large dorsal and anal fins toward the rear of its body give strong takeoff power for lightning strikes, but decrease maneuverability. Thus the pike will shun a darting baitfish (or lure) in favor of one that follows a straight course.

they have become masters of camouflage and lie in weed beds as still as a log until the moment of strike. Nor are pike well-suited to operate in the swift waters of rivers. With steering leverage at the rear, a pike cannot easily hold its head up into the current.

If you look at a pike, one of the first things you'll notice is that the eyes are located near the top of the head, giving them good overhead vision. Thus, they prefer to lie low and strike on an angle toward the surface. Their whole method of propulsion and body shape are tailored to seeing food above them and then striking out like a coiled rattler. It's easy to see why surface lures or topwater poppers are an excellent choice for members of this family.

The black basses have an entirely different form than the pikes and from this we would expect them to have a different mode of propulsion. Both the smallmouth and the large-mouth bass are stockier than the pikes. The fins of the basses are more evenly spread along the body with much more fin surface toward the front of the body. This gives them excellent maneuverability at pursuit speed and a talent for chasing down elusive prey. The large head and mouth improve their chances of engulfing their prey on the run when they are within range.

Bass are admirably suited for cruising among logs, rocks, and undergrowth, where they hide and forage for food. Their broad fins and strong, stout body enable them to take any position and go in any direction (even backwards) as they poke around looking for crawfish and other prey. They are said to have the strength to turn over rocks in their search for food and enjoy a propulsion system that makes them extremely versatile.

In contrast to the pike, the black bass is a stocky fish with more fin surface toward the front of its body. The bass can maneuver at high speed and will strike a baitfish or lure moving in an erratic pattern; but it does not excel at long, fast pursuits.

Built for the fast strike, though lacking the maneuverability of the bass, the trout exhibits the classic fish form. Placement of eyes toward the front of head gives this fish good forward and upward vision for sighting underwater or topwater insects.

This versatility makes the bass a natural for almost any type of artificial lure. No matter how the bait cavorts through the water, the bass responds quickly, turning and darting in close pursuit. On the other hand, the bass is not a fish geared for long, fast pursuit. The bait has to be presented fairly close to the lie of the fish and then moved at a slow or moderate speed. Pike might bolt after a speedy offering, but the large-mouth generally prefers to look it over and then crash it. The strike might be explosive, but the approach seldom is.

In body form, fin type, and mode of propulsion, the trouts fall in between the pikes and basses. They have the moderate-sized head and the elongated body that exemplifies the classic fish form. With most of their fin surface on the rearward half of their bodies, trout exhibit excellent striking power. Yet, the trout is compact enough to hold in a strong current much better than a pike. Although they will some-times "mouth" a nymph, they are geared to the fast strike, swallowing their prey directly. A relatively large head and mouth makes this possible, and therefore, trout don't need the long, sharp teeth of the pike.

Placement of a trout's eyes show that it has perfect straight-ahead vision to pinpoint prey and moderately good upward vision to watch for surface action from a lair. The general structure of the trout suggests that they are fish of moderate speed, good striking power, and high stamina geared to take their prey in the open. A degree of agility characterizes their performance, but they do not have the maneuverability of the bass.

What we have said about propulsion of the pikes, basses, and trouts applies rather directly to their counterpart saltwater species. The barracuda resembles the pike and will react in similar fashion. Groupers and largemouth bass exhibit the same forms of propulsion and thus the habits are almost identical. Similarly, the seatrouts and freshwater trouts share body form and behavioral characteristics.

The larger the fish, the faster it can swim. As a rule of thumb, you can calculate the top cruising speed of most fish at the rate of 7 miles per hour for each foot of length. A 6-inch fish would be able to swim at about 3½ miles per hour; an 18-inch fish at 10½ miles per hour. There are many exceptions to this rule, of course, because the speed varies greatly from species to species depending on form and muscle power. Another interesting generalization is that burst speeds are about 50 percent higher than the maximum sustainable speeds. Thus, a salmon with a top sustained speed of 10 miles per hour could reach a burst speed of 15 miles per hour before leaving the water to leap over a waterfall or on that first dash after feeling the barb of the fly.

At the sustained rate, a fish can energize its muscles and remove the wastes from them via the bloodstream, continuously at a balanced rate. At high burst speeds, poisonous lactic acid builds up rapidly in the muscles. Experiments with salmon have shown that lactic acid can kill fish by slow internal poisoning within a few hours after overexertion. This applies equally to the energy expended by a hooked fish fighting for its very existence. Therefore, if you plan to release the fish, use heavy enough tackle and don't play it longer than is absolutely necessary. Otherwise, it may swim away happily but die in a few hours from lactic acid poisoning.

Fish naturally attempt to conserve energy by controlling its output. Once a salmon, fighting its way upstream to spawn, has cleared the falls, it would probably be found resting in a quiet pool for awhile to balance its internal chemistry. Depending on size, a salmon is capable of sustained speeds of 7 to 10 miles per *hour*, yet the actual progress of the salmon's upstream migration is much slower—perhaps 7 to 10 miles per *day*.

Biologists have a difficult time setting up laboratory experiments to measure top speeds of fish. But, in natural waters, some observations have been taken and top speeds have been estimated. Largemouth and striped bass have been clocked at

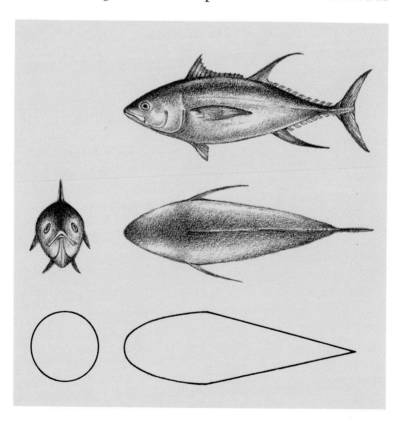

Endowed with a perfect fusiform shape, the tuna (left) and the blue crevalle (above) are nearly round in cross section and taper smoothly toward both ends. Both fish are built to meet minimum water resistance at high speeds. Their streamlining could not be improved by an engineer.

Top Speed Estimates	
Species	*Burst Speed*
Bass, largemouth	12
Bass, smallmouth	12
Bass, striped	12
Salmon	14
Barracuda	28
Dolphin	37
Bonito	40+
Marlin	40+
Tuna	50
Sailfish	60
Swordfish	60

12 miles per hour, mackerel at 20½, dolphin at 37, and tuna at more than 50 miles per hour. The table on page 22 lists some of these speeds.

Because the tuna's specialty is speed, its body is a solid mass of muscle with other structures held to a minimum. The bluefin tuna, for example, has nearly the smallest abdomen of all oceanic fishes, with the whole mass comprising only 3 or 4 percent of its weight. The head is only large enough to house essential sensory organs and a set of gills of sufficient size to provide oxygen to the powerful muscles. Like many other oceanic surface fishes, bluefins do not pump water over their gills, but simply open their mouths a bit as they swim, forcing water to pass over the gills and out the rear flap.

The bluefin has two kinds of body muscle to meet its two different needs: a mass of white muscle for short-distance, high-speed swimming and a small amount of dark muscle for prolonged low-speed swimming. Open a can of white-meat tuna and you can see these flaky, high-speed muscles. The masses of white muscle that make up most of its body give the bluefin tuna the speed it needs to run down its prey or to avoid its chief enemy, the killer whale. The dark muscle, running from head to tail in a band along the center line of the bluefin, is heavily supplied with blood and can operate continuously without fatigue, providing the endurance the tuna needs to migrate thousands of miles in its annual travels.

Tuna also demonstrate the extreme in body form. A hydro-dynamics engineer could not have designed a form that is more perfectly shaped to move smoothly through the water at high speeds with the least possible resistance. Nearly round in cross section and tapering smoothly toward both ends, with maximum girth one-third of the way back from the nose, tuna have the perfect fusiform shape. Although this is the general form found in most species, fish that do not spe-cialize in high-speed swimming, such as the perch or sunfish, tend to have a less perfect streamlined shape and are flatter for greater ease in undulating and flexing the body.

JET PROPULSION

There are some other tricks that fish use in moving them-selves. Jet action from the gills enters into the propulsion of fishes. In normal breathing, water passes through the mouth and over the gills. It is then expelled backwards through the gill flaps, giving some forward thrust to aid swimming. A fish at rest has to offset this forward thrust by gently back pedal-ing with its pectoral fins.

Many fish are known to use jet propulsion for quicker start-ing. Flounders are especially adept at jet-assisted takeoffs. By expelling hard out of the lower gill flap, they can simulta-neously rise off the bottom and thrust forward at good speed. Once off and away, they start normal propulsion, which, in the ultra-thin flounder, consists of up and down undulations of the body together with rhythmic movements of the ample fins which almost encircle the body.

However, the main value of the jet action to fish appears to be in the lessening of skin resistance to the water. Most of this resistance, or drag, that the water exerts on the fish's body occurs back of the shoulder. Because the gill flap ends at the shoulder, the water expelled from the gill chamber passes smoothly over the skin and lessens the drag. Techni-

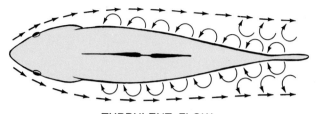

TURBULENT FLOW

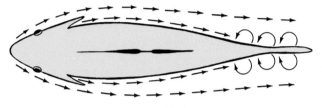

LAMINAR FLOW

Fish are endowed with a kind of jet propulsion. Water passes through the mouth and out the gills, giving forward thrust and a laminar flow along the body. In the top drawing, the curved arrows show what would happen if a fish had no gills for water passage: water passing over the shoulder would create a turbulent flow along the body and cause drag. In the bottom drawing, water passes through the gills in a laminar flow along the body (straight arrows), with a slight turbulence near the tail, and causes minimum drag.

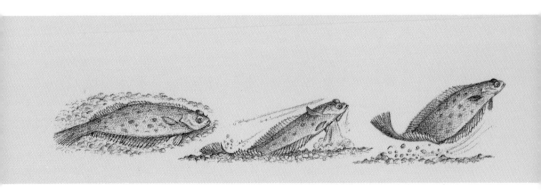

Lying flat on the ocean floor, the flounder shoots water through its gills for a jet assisted takeoff (JATO). Since one of the flounder's gills is in contact with the bottom, the jet stream hits a solid surface and gives the fish a powerful boost.

cally, a "laminar" flow replaces the "turbulent" flow, enabling the fish to swim faster for the same amount of energy output. To complete the story, of some 300 species checked for this characteristic, 90 percent had their gill flaps at the exact theoretical point for maximum jet-flow streamlining.

Experiments just completed show that many species, including smallmouth bass, trout, and barracuda, excrete a special slime that dissolves away layer by layer as the fish swim at high speeds, thus reducing friction and turbulence. The frictional drag is reduced by 65.9 percent for Pacific barracuda, and about 60 percent for rainbow or brown trout. Even crappie and bluegill benefit from the special type of slime. Some tuna-like speedsters, such as bonito, do not have this slime but have overcome the need for it by their special forms and modes of propulsion.

Fish can be divided into two groups according to their fin type. The sea bass is an example of a spiny-rayed fish, the rainbow trout of a soft-rayed fish. In general, soft-rayed fish jump, spiny-rays don't.

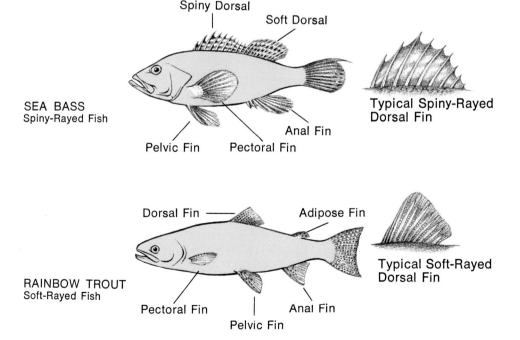

Spiny Dorsal

Soft Dorsal

SEA BASS
Spiny-Rayed Fish

Typical Spiny-Rayed
Dorsal Fin

Pelvic Fin   Pectoral Fin

Anal Fin

Dorsal Fin ———   Adipose Fin

RAINBOW TROUT
Soft-Rayed Fish

Typical Soft-Rayed
Dorsal Fin

Pectoral Fin   Anal Fin

Pelvic Fin

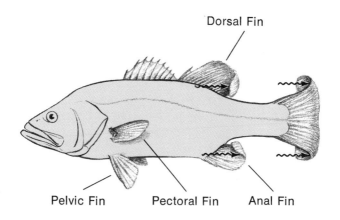

Dorsal Fin

Pelvic Fin   Pectoral Fin   Anal Fin

Fish use their fins for braking, extending pectorals outward, curling dorsal and anal fins in one direction, and the tail fin in the other. Using all fins in this way helps the fish to stabilize itself when it brakes.

HOW FISH USE THEIR FINS

A few slow-moving species use their fins for swimming, but most fish use them primarily for stabilization, maneuvering, and various other special tasks. In fact, the faster-swimming fish usually retract their fins when they want to speed up, dropping them back into slots or depressions so that they virtually disappear.

The paired pectoral fins can be extended as planers, enabling the fish to dive if the fins are tipped down or to climb if they are tipped up. This is the same principle as the bowplanes on a submarine that control the angle of ascent or descent. The pectorals can also be extended one at a time, like an oar, to help the fish turn right or left. Pelvic fins, also paired, play a similar but less important role.

The unpaired fins, dorsals and anals, are used mainly as keels to prevent rocking motions and to keep the fish straight up during swimming, particularly at lower speeds. At top speed, a fish is able to maintain a balanced course without much help from these fins.

The fins not only promote fast starts and rapid turns, but they permit quick stops when both the pectorals and pelvics are thrust out suddenly. If a fish like the largemouth used its pelvics and pectorals alone, all the stopping resistance would

Flaring its pectoral fins and curving its tail, a rockfish veers to the right and cuts its speed as it approaches an underwater reef.

be added forward and to the lower side of the fish, causing it to tip up from the tail if it tried to stop in a hurry. To counter this force, other fins are brought into play. Sometimes, the rearward tips of the dorsal, anal, and tail fins are curved back to add counterbalancing resistance to the rearward and higher parts of the fish, allowing for a more balanced stop. Pikes do not have an extreme tip-up problem in stopping because their broad pelvic fins, set well back on the underside, counteract the force of the pectorals.

In general, fish can be divided into two groups: spiny-rayed fish that have spines in one or more fins, and soft-rayed fish that have no spines in their fins.

Shattering the face of a tranquil sea, a mighty sailfish makes a vain leap for freedom as the angler pumps it steadily toward the boat. The sailfish jumps even when it's not fighting for its life—for example, to dislodge foreign matter from its bill. When hooked, it merely relies on familiar behavior patterns.

JUMPING FISH

The biggest thrill in angling comes when a fish leaves the
water in a dazzling display of aerial acrobatics, tailwalking
and gyrating to throw the hook. It is equally exciting to look
across the water and observe a fish you are chasing suddenly
bolt skyward in pursuit of natural bait. The king mackerel
often "skyrockets" on the strike, leaping almost 20 feet in the
air. Other members of the mackerel family will leave the
water to pounce on a surface bait 25 feet away.

Anglers often feel that a fish will tire itself by jumping, but
this does not appear to be borne out by the facts. A fish
moving fast in the water is released to become a virtual
rocket when it breaks the surface. It is as if someone opens
the door suddenly while you are pushing on it. The propel-
ling force comes from the momentum of rapid swimming
upward, climaxed by a strong thrust of the tail just as the fish
leaves the water. Therefore, to be a high jumper, a fish must
be a fast swimmer and have a strong tail.

A case in point is the porpoise (bottlenose dolphin). If
you've ever been to a seaquarium and watched these graceful
leapers take food out of a trainer's hand, you know how
effortlessly they seem to rise. Watch the jumping porpoise
from underwater and you'll see that it swims along at a good
speed and then, with a last flip of the tail, propels itself
upward and out of the water.

In general, the soft-rayed fishes are jumpers and the spiny-
rayed fishes are not. But there are exceptions, such as spiny-
rayed fish like the smallmouth bass that jump and soft-rayed
fish like the bonefish that do not jump.

Strict bottom feeders are not natural jumpers and would
not jump if hooked. Fish that do jump when hooked are
usually surface feeding natural jumpers. Trout and salmon
can be observed jumping free and barracuda and sailfish will
do the same. Exceptions include pike and snook, which do
not jump naturally but do take to the air when hooked and
the Spanish mackerel tribe, which jump naturally but fight
underwater.

When a fish is hooked it is up against a new experience and all it can do is fall back on its natural skills. In its panic, it will try everything it knows. If it is a deep swimmer it will dive. If it is a sprinter, it will sprint. If it is a reef dweller, it will run for a cave. And if it is a jumper, it will jump.

THE SWIM BLADDER

Hovering in mid-water is an action that presents difficulties to fish because they are heavier than water and tend to sink. Many species must be able to maintain a steady position somewhere between bottom and surface for hours. To enable fish to accomplish this, nature has provided them with a swim bladder in the abdominal cavity just below the backbone and above the stomach. The swim bladder is basically a hollow, air-tight sac, analogous to the human lung, that is used to

Deflating or inflating a swim bladder in the abdominal cavity helps a fish maintain the proper buoyancy to hold itself at any depth. The swim bladder must be located at the fish's exact center of gravity; if not, the fish would be destabilized, as shown in the first three drawings. Fortunately, nature has provided most fish with a centered swim bladder (Fig. 4).

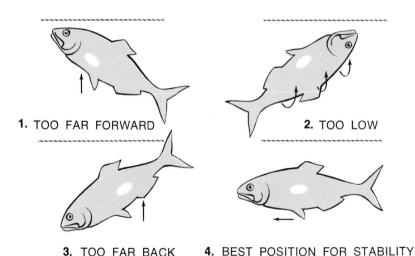

1. TOO FAR FORWARD   **2.** TOO LOW

3. TOO FAR BACK   **4.** BEST POSITION FOR STABILITY

control flotation. By pumping it up or deflating it, the fish
can achieve just the right amount of buoyancy to offset
gravity. Then, with a minimum of fin action, the fish can
hold itself in position.

A trout can stay just under the surface to lie in wait for
insects; a pickerel can hide in a grass bed with a minimum of
alarm-giving fin motions; a bass can stay over its nest for
hours to protect its young without tiring. The most efficient
swim bladders are those located most nearly at the center of
gravity of the body so the fish is in balance when completely
inactive.

If the swim bladder is too far forward or backward, the fish
will tend to tip up or down. If it is too low, the fish will tend
to roll over and float belly up. To correct any imbalance, a
fish must use up its energy in fin motion. Fortunately, nature
has put the swim bladder near the center of gravity of most
fish to minimize the amount of corrective fin action necessary. Remember that a fish must use fin motion to counteract
the jet thrust created by the water flowing through the gills
and along its body. The best swim bladder arrangement bal-
ances this fin motion against the center of gravity.

Some species sacrifice perfect balance for other advantages. One fish, the upside-down catfish, solved its problem
by learning to swim on its back, which is the normal posture
for this species. The salmon has its swim bladder, and therefore its center of buoyancy, below its center of gravity and
uses this relationship to advantage in banking on turns. The
lower center of buoyancy tends to roll the fish up sideways, a
disadvantage when hovering, but an advantage when turning
in a current. This pays off particularly when the salmon
chases bait to the surface and wants to dive back down as
quickly as possible. The salmon, like most species, doesn't
bend well vertically, but does flex easily from side to side.
Therefore its best strategy is to roll 90 degrees over on its side
just as it reaches the surface and curve its body in a downward arc. Technically called flexed rotation, the thrust of the
lunge toward the surface is reversed and the momentum of
the fish forces it downward immediately. In contrast, less

active feeders like the yellow perch have the center of buoyancy above the center of gravity.

It is vitally important for a fisherman to understand this
rotation and fully comprehend that a fish often turns on its
side under the surface and returns to the depths. In this type
of situation, the tail often breaks the surface of the water or a
large boil occurs. To the uninitiated, it appears that the fish is
feeding on the surface, and the natural instinct is to use a
top-water fly or lure.

In reality, the fish is feeding *below* the surface and the
commotion seen is nothing more than the swirl caused by the
tail of the fish as it returns to its lie or continues cruising at
normal depth. We've witnessed this clearly in a large laboratory tank watching bluefish feed on live bait. The fish is several feet from the boil and heading away from it by the time
the disturbance is visible on the surface.

Without exception, freshwater fish that do not have swim
bladders are bottom dwellers. It is obvious that fish whose
home is on the bottom are not in need of buoyancy. In this
case buoyancy would be a hindrance and there is no need
for a swim bladder. When they want to rest, they merely
settle down on the bottom.

It is not surprising that saltwater bottom species like flounders lack swim bladders, but there is a contrast with freshwater species in that salt water surface fishes sometimes lack a
swim bladder. The Atlantic mackerel is always in motion,
and since it never rests, it gets by perfectly without a swim
bladder. This member of the mackerel family makes up for
the pull of gravity by applying a slight but constant upward
thrust while swimming. Tunas are also constant swimmers
and either have a reduced bladder or none at all. Sharks, too,
are without a swim bladder, relying partly on the large
amount of oil in their livers for flotation.

The swim bladder is larger in freshwater fish because there
is no salt in the water to buoy them up. In freshwater fish, the
swim bladder occupies 7 to 11 percent of body volume, as
opposed to only 4 to 6 percent in saltwater fish.

Although a swim bladder is an advantage in most respects,

it can be a marked disadvantage in others. If a fish moves up quickly from the depths, the air in the swim bladder expands, adding to the fish's buoyancy and thus to the upward force. In accordance with Boyle's Law, half of the pressure in the bladder is removed for each 30 feet of rise. If the air sac were fully expandable, it would double in size when brought to the surface from 30 feet and quadruple in size from 60 feet to the surface. In reality, however, the bladder does not usually expand this much, because the air within it is held at a higher pressure. Nevertheless, it does expand enough to prevent a fish from easily returning to its original depth.

If a fish with a swim bladder goes up too far, too fast, the critical point is passed and the fish may lose control and be carried helplessly to the surface. It the bladder has not been ruptured, and if other vital parts have not been damaged, fish can, in time, get rid of the air in their swim bladder through the bloodstream. At that point, they can regain control and return to the depths. Saltwater fish typically have a duct that connects the bladder directly to the throat, allowing them to burp air out fast enough on their way up to avoid the ballooning effect. Freshwater species do not have this duct and suffer greater limitation on their vertical movements.

Since the swim bladder is like a lung, think about this example: A diver, adjusted to air pressure at the surface, can dive rather quickly to depths of 200 feet or more with negligible effects because of the flexibility of his ribs and other body parts. But a diver adjusted to the pressure at 200 feet (or even 50 feet) would explode like a bomb if he were pulled to the surface rapidly, unless he could blow out enough air through his mouth to compensate for the reduced pressure. Most fish can't do this. In the example of the diver, we are discussing air expansion and not the "bends," which result from gas in the blood coming out of solution and expanding into large bubbles which stop circulation.

Open-ocean fish that dive deep after prey would find the contractions and expansions of the swim bladder a nuisance. That is why tunas, sharks, and swordfish do not have a swim bladder. There are no freshwater counterparts of these species because freshwater surface fish do not dive to such great depths after prey.

Emphasis has been placed on the swim bladder because it offers a great deal of information about how a fish will react when hooked. Knowing what to expect from your quarry will help to even the odds in bringing a fish to net or gaff. At this point, you should be aware that any fish with a developed swim bladder cannot change depth quickly and certainly not at burst speed. Thus, it must remain in the zone in which it is hooked.

In a specific example, experiments show that the European perch swimming at a depth of 60 feet can only dive to 72 feet or rise to 48 feet (a 20 percent change in depth) comfortably. Any deeper or shallower movement will put the fish out of control. The tolerances on most species are not this critical, and although most can dive easily, they do encounter serious difficulty in trying to surface rapidly. Tuna and billfish in salt water will often carry the fight to the bottom and simply refuse to budge. Then, with a suddenness of purpose, they will rush to the surface. The majority of species, however, do not enjoy the advantage of lacking a swim bladder, and once they are down, you have to force them to the surface.

If you are trolling deep in a large lake and happen to hook a lake trout, northern pike, or even a salmon, don't expect the fish to display the same fighting characteristics as it would if it struck on the surface. The swim bladder is conditioned to that depth and that is where the fight will take place. The fish will "dig in" and try to stay within its comfort range. Your job is to try to turn its head upward and force it toward the surface. The instant the fish rises faster than the air in the bladder can be dissipated, the bladder will expand and the fish will go out of control. It feels as if your adversary has given up.

In many species, the swim bladder is modified to provide special functions in addition to buoyancy control. The sea trout and haddock have bladders with built-in devices for producing the mating call. This phenomenon occurs only in males and is used in the breeding season to attract the females. In the tarpon and gar, there is a connecting tube to the throat from the bladder which enables the swim bladder to serve as a lung by taking in air and providing oxygen to the fish's blood beyond what the gills can supply. These species can survive in polluted water that has little or no oxygen by simply breathing air. They can also expel air quickly by burping, and you can often see the bubbles rising to the surface.

FIGHTING AND LANDING FISH

The shape of any fish and its propulsion system give you an immediate clue to its behavior when hooked. A speedy, open-water fish will usually strike fast and is designed for longer pursuit but less maneuverability. Species that take up residence around reefs or underwater obstructions are slower, and although they may hit a bait or lure quickly, they will seldom pursue it far from their lair. Frequently, a fish will realize that it is more difficult to make headway against a drag by running straight away. The pressure seems to be slightly less on a quartering angle and the fish can use its body as a buffer to keep you from forcing it closer to the boat or shore. This is a favorite technique of broad-beamed fish such as members of the Jack family, and even the largemouth bass will employ this method.

When a fish leaves the safety of the depths, it is looking for food, and this is one of the easiest times to elicit a strike. The response of any hooked species is to run for deep water. Knowing this ahead of time, you can anticipate a long first run and almost pinpoint the direction that the fish will take. The drag on the reel can be set lighter than normal so that there will be no chance of the drag binding as the line clears the reel on the initial dash. If you can stop the fish before it reaches deep water, you stand a better chance of landing it sooner, but count on your adversary to make repeated attempts to reach the dropoff.

If there is one time when it is important to be on your toes, it is when the fish is close to being landed. You can bet that the fish will make a final dash the instant he sees boat, shore, net, or gaff. The best technique is to let him go and actually point your rod at him to lessen the pressure on the drag. This will compensate for the sudden surge. The instant the reel spool begins to give line, raise the rod back to the fighting position again. Some species when caught from a boat will look upon the vessel as a form of cover or protection and dive underneath it. Often, on an inboard, they will cut right across the shaft and propeller. In this event, your only chance is to push the rod in the water as far as you can reach and lead the line safely around the stern to the other side.

Slipping a net under your catch or trying to gaff a fish can be achieved much easier if you stop to consider the fish's propulsion system. Even beaching a fish or dragging it up on shore can be simplified if you make the propulsion system work for you. Remember that a fish cannot swim backward very well. Some species can back-pedal slowly, but a fish is designed to move forward and every tail movement will drive it ahead.

Netting a fish is much easier than gaffing, because you have a larger target to work with. The object is to place the net in the water at a 45-degree angle with the top of the webbing just above the surface, then lead the fish into the net head first. Any sudden movement or tail beat will only serve to drive the fish into the net. If a fish is built to maneuver easily, and you try to scoop it up in the net, it will turn away quickly and you run the risk of breaking the leader or knocking the fish off the hook.

A gaff is much more difficult to use, but there are some guidelines. Almost all experienced gaffers have their own techniques and stick to them. Some will reach across the back of the fish; others will place the gaff in the water or under the belly of the fish and have the angler lead the fish over the gaff. Since you cannot move a net or gaff through the water quickly, the fish should be on the surface or close to it. One tip of importance from a master with the gaff can make it easier for you. He follows two basic rules. The first is that he never brings the gaff past the head and eyes of the fish; otherwise, the fish will see it and dart off. Even more important, when he plants the gaff, this skipper makes certain that the head of the fish is pointing away from the boat. Then, if he does miss or the fish surges, the momentum will carry the fish away from the boat and not underneath it where the line could get cut.

Many an angler makes the mistake of backing away from the gunwale of the boat or from the shoreline just when the fish is ready for net or gaff. Often, this deprives him of a good view of the proceedings, and a sudden surge by the fish will catch him off guard. The proper procedure is to stay in fighting position. If anything, move closer.

Landing a fish in the surf by beaching it or dragging it up on a gravel bar is relatively simple, but again, you should let the fish do the work for you. Avoid letting the fish drag along the bottom in shallow water where the hook could pull out. Let the fish swim in the shallows with your guidance. Then force it to the surface and slide it up on the gravel bar in one continuous sweep. This should be a smooth effort and not a series of jerks or pulls. Don't try to lift the fish out of the water, merely surfboard it across the top.

In the surf, the problem is slightly different. Waves move toward the beach and then recede. Most surf-caught fish have broad bodies that enable them to chase bait in the breakers, and the force of a receding wave against this shape can cause extra strain on the tackle. A skillful surf fisherman works the fish toward the breaker line, keeping the fish directly in front of him. The beginner makes the mistake of letting the fish run parallel to the beach while he stays in one spot. When this happens, just move down the beach with your fish, keeping it directly seaward from where you are standing at the moment.

As the fish tires and works toward the surface, use the waves to swim it toward you. Try to get it on the crest of a wave and pump fast, dragging it toward the beach. As that wave passes, pause until the next one picks up the fish. Repeat the procedure until the fish is almost at your feet and the water is barely deep enough to support it. Then, wait for a good wave, get the fish up on top, and run right out of the surf, pulling the fish with you. The receding wave should leave it high and dry.

3

Seeing

To catch a fish, you must first catch its eye. Sound and smell may cause an initial response, but when most gamefish make their final attack on your offering they are guided solely by eyesight. Understanding the importance of eyesight in fish behavior, and how a fish actually sees underwater, can help an angler in many ways.

HOW FISH ADJUST TO LIGHT

The typical fish eye is remarkably akin to the human eye. The similarity may seem surprising when you consider that man lives in an environment of air while a fish lives in water, but the principles of eyesight are much the same throughout the animal kingdom.

A fish's eye is a camera. Light rays enter the eye and are picked up by the lens, the transparent center of the eyeball. The lens directs the light rays to the back of the eye and focuses them on a light-sensitive screen, called the retina.

In our own eye we have an iris, or diaphragm, in front of the lens that opens or closes down depending on the amount of light entering the eye. The iris in a fish's eye is fixed. It is an opaque curtain of tissue with a hole in the center. The iris admits light through the fixed center aperture only, while blocking out light coming in from beyond the edges of the fish's field of vision. Adjustments to changes in the brightness of light are managed by receptor cells in the retina.

There are two types of receptor cells in the retina which are used alternately, depending on light levels: rod cells and cone cells. Each group sends messages to the brain describing any image that is flashed on the retina. The cone cells are the color receptors of the fish and are used in daytime or whenever the light source is brighter than about one foot-candle. At night, or when the light level falls below one foot-candle, fish change over to the rod cells, which are the super light-sensitive receptors. In fact, the rods are about thirty times more sensitive than the cones, but they detect and record only black and white.

During periods of brightness, the cones are pushed to the surface of the retina and the rod receptors are withdrawn deep into it where dark pigments protect these sensitive cells from damage by bright light.

Scientists have found that the change from daytime vision with cones to nighttime vision with rods does not happen instantaneously. The complete changeover may occupy two hours or more in the fish's normal daily cycle. As an example, experiments with bluegills have shown that it ordinarily takes two to three hours after sunset for the rods to extend and adjust fully to darkness. When the rods are completely extended, they remain in that position for only about two hours. Then the process reverses itself. The rods begin to retract slowly and the cones gradually are extended in preparation for the coming of the morning light. This is a fully automatic process that works with amazing regularity. Somehow, the fish "remembers" how long it is from sunset to sunup, setting its internal alarm clock to remind the cells to move at the right time so that everything is set and ready to go at dawn.

If the sun were to set at 6 P.M. and rise at 6 A.M., the bluegill would be fully adapted to dark by 8 or 9 P.M. It would remain this way until 10 or 11 P.M., and then gradually adjust for the coming of light the next morning. The same sequence occurs during daylight hours as the fish begins adjusting for the coming of darkness far in advance. The details of adaptation in the retina will vary from fish to fish, but we can safely assume that most predators that feed primarily by sight go through a relatively slow process of adjusting their vision each morning and evening.

Understanding that it takes time for a fish to adjust to different light conditions can help the angler in many ways. When a fish is night adjusted, any sudden illumination of the strength equal to even that of a cloudy day can "burn" the sensitive rod cells. The experiments with bluegills showed that when hit with a sudden light, these fish would sink to the bottom of the tank and remain immobile, or they would swim around in a disoriented manner.

The degree of light shock depends upon how exposed the rod cells are; that is, how far into night adaptation the fish has gone. Shock may last five minutes or longer in a fish that is fully dark adapted, but it will last only about two minutes in a fish that is partially adapted—say, just after night fall or just before dawn. You can prove this to yourself very easily. Take a powerful flashlight and play it over the surface of the water until you pick up a fish in the beam. Hold the beam on the fish and it will go into light shock, with one of two results depending on the species. The fish may panic and try to escape the beam of light, or it may be attracted by the light and become hypnotized, remaining motionless and helpless.

It is therefore important to avoid using artificial lights at night in most fishing situations. There is a natural tendency to want to see at night, and anglers sometimes try to brighten the area for their own ease in moving about. But this can have an adverse effect on the fish. Another common failing is to drive up to the water's edge, allowing the headlights from the car or beach buggy to fall across the surface. You're far better off when working in darkness to use artificial light sparingly.

Another effect of artificial light on fish may be seen under a permanent dock light at night. The light attracts tiny plankton which concentrate in the bright spot, setting up a feeding arena for baitfish that come in to forage on the plankton.

Gamefish lurking in the shadows raid the baitfish that hover in the light. This is particularly true of tarpon and snook in the Florida Keys. But these fish have already adjusted their eyes to the light, and the adjustment has taken place over a period of time. That's why there is better fishing if you leave the same light on every night, whether or not you plan to fish. If you throw a sudden light directly on fish, they will flee in fear more times than not.

FEEDING AND LIGHT ADJUSTMENT

The most successful feeders are the fish whose eyesight-adjusting process is in rhythm with the natural cycles of night and day. The fish that is bright-eyed and ready for the early-morning light will get the jump on its prey. The same holds true for evening. Because many gamefish have exceedingly good light adjustment, they have an advantage when light levels are low or marginal and they prefer to feed at this time. That is why fishing is usually good at daybreak and again at dusk.

This is a predictable schedule for other reasons, too. Just as you get up in the morning hungry, so does a fish. Because fish take up to half a day to digest their food, a fish that is sated in the early morning is probably ready to feed once more in the late afternoon and again the following morning. This pattern continues day after day.

In marginal light, a gamefish can stalk its prey with higher efficiency than in full light. To make a gain, fish have to weigh the energy expended against the rewards harvested. It is a simple fact that they expend less energy hunting in marginal light, so that is the time when they feed heavily. If you have ever been on the water just before daybreak, you may have been disappointed by the lack of strikes. Then, as the sky lightens in the east, the fish start to strike. The same reaction may occur again at dusk.

Even the weather plays a part, and the habitat of the species must also be considered. Fish feed at different times on clear and cloudy days. Surface-feeding fish might start earlier than those species living in the depths. Active feeding in the

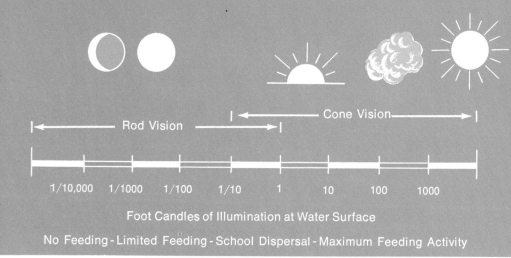

Rod Vision

Cone Vision

| 1/10,000 | 1/1000 | 1/100 | 1/10 | 1 | 10 | 100 | 1000 |

Foot Candles of Illumination at Water Surface

No Feeding - Limited Feeding - School Dispersal - Maximum Feeding Activity

This chart shows the feeding activity of salmon in relation to the amount of light on the surface of the water. At night, when fish rely on rod vision (left side of graph), little or no feeding activity was observed. But as light on the surface of the water increases, and cone vision takes over (right side), feeding activity also increases.

subdued light of morning and evening is especially prevalent in the shallows because the larger gamefish can enter thin water in low light with a margin of safety from detection.

No one has worked out the details of how rapidly a fish can adjust to light changes when swimming up from murky depths to the upper layers, but it is quite probable that fish swimming rapidly to the surface from the darker depths suffer momentary blindness. In our own experiences, we could liken it to walking out of a movie theater into bright daylight. The reverse, of course, would be a fish near the surface in the daytime diving down into deeper water to feed. Since the fish would be on cone vision, he would see poorly in the dimness of the depths.

WATER CLARITY AND VISION

Water clarity is an important factor in vision because it controls the amount of light that penetrates through the water and the distance that a fish can see. Even in a very clear lake such as Crystal Lake, Wisconsin, 99 percent of the light is filtered out in the first 27 feet below the surface. In murky lakes, most of the light is gone in the first 10 feet. Still, if sunshine is illuminating the surface at 2,000 foot-candles there will be 20 foot-candles at the depth where only one percent of the light remains, plenty of light for fish to feed by.

Because even the purest water is a poorer conductor of light than is air, visibility underwater is limited to a few hundred feet under the very best conditions. But the turbidity of most fishing waters—caused by plankton and silt particles—reduces visibility to between 5 and 40 feet. The particles in the water scatter the light and block its passage just as smoke or fog does in the air. Unless a fish is alerted to the approach of a lure by sound, it may have only a fleeting moment to react when the lure suddenly appears. That is why spoons and plugs that are built to "flash" produce results under turbid conditions.

However, in some waters and under some conditions, the sudden flash of a large artificial may have the reverse effect. Unless the flash appears to be from a natural baitfish, it could frighten the gamester rather than attract it. Instinctively, the fish knows it is either food or an enemy and its reaction depends on what the flash appears to be. For the fish, a mistake could be fatal.

Salmon and trout can feed in an exceptionally wide range of illumination. These species hunt with their eyes, chasing down their prey and swallowing them head first. In the evening, as the light fades below one foot-candle, the trouts and salmons have switched from cone to rod vision and usually cease their normal manner of feeding. However, that's also the time for fresh hatches of insects to appear on the surface of the water, silhouetted against the sky and making an easy target.

Knowing this, the fly fisherman doesn't have to be concerned with matching the hatch exactly. The trick is to produce a silhouette of the right size and light value. Depending on this light value, your fly will show up as dark or light against the sky—the fine color shadings normally associated with flies are lost in the low light levels. If you can get an idea of the size of the natural and whether it is dark or light, you should do as well with any pattern you have of the same size and light value. A trout in the twilight cannot discern the exact color before it commits itself.

Big brown trout are notorious for foraging the shallows after dark in search of minnows. Sound plays a key role in helping the brownies to find their prey, and anglers have done well on popping flies and bugs. Arnold Hubbell of Mio, Michigan, has accounted for more big brown trout after dark than any man we know. Hub insists that it is extremely important to "splat" a fly on the surface to get the fish's attention. Feeding brown trout at night don't require a delicate, dry-fly type of presentation. In fact, fly patterns streaked with reflective mylar often make the task easier. Brownies must isolate their prey for the kill, and the silver flash created by the mylar helps them to home in on their target.

Silhouettes play a part in the use of topwater baits in both fresh water and salt. An ocean-traveling gamefish is looking up at a bait skipping behind the boat, and this means that the bait will be silhouetted. Size, shape, and light value again become significant. Think in terms of contrasting light values rather than specific colors. Consider the dark or light water and sky. Then choose a topwater bait that will stand out sharply when viewed from below. This is also true during low light hours and when the water is rough or turbid. On a rough day, experienced offshore fishermen will lean toward a bigger bait than on a calm day, because it will be more visible among the whitecaps. Others favor a swimming bait rather than a skipbait on those days. The reasoning is the same.

WHY FISH ARE NEARSIGHTED

You may have heard that fish are myopic (nearsighted). The eye of a fish is round rather than flattened like ours, and it cannot change focus by adjusting its shape. The round lens causes shortsightedness, but a fish really doesn't need long-range vision because the visibility in water is usually poor. Therefore, many fish rely on their other senses to locate prey

initially and use their eyes only at short range for the final
strike.

Although fish cannot flatten their lenses to focus on distant
objects as we do, they are able to move the lenses closer to
the retina, which helps to accomplish the same thing to some
degree. This is done by contraction of a small muscle (the
retractor lentis) which hooks on the bottom of the lens and
pulls it back. Because the lens is already set for close-up
vision when the muscle is at rest, there is no need for reverse
action.

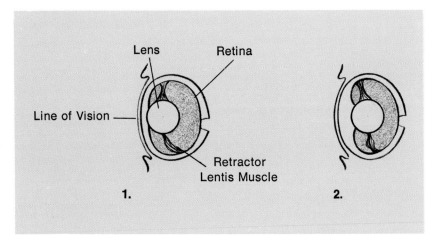

To focus on distant objects, a fish can move its lens closer to the retina by means of the retractor lentis muscle. When the muscle is at rest
(Fig. 1), the lens is focused at close-range objects. In Fig. 2, the muscle has pulled the lens closer to the retina for long-range vision.

Sight feeders such as the brown trout have excellent
powers of lens movement—that is, they have a strong retractor muscle. They also have other refinements of the lens and
retina which enable them to focus on objects both near and
far at the same time. By reading the separate images on separate parts of the retina, they gain a sort of simultaneous
bifocal vision. This is possible because their lens is shaped
like an egg with the pointed end aimed at the retina.

RANGE OF SIGHT

Since their eyes are placed on the sides of their heads, fish have a wide range of sight. But the right and left eyes each see a separate half of the field and they suffer a bit from split vision. Nevertheless, it is an advantage to have each eye able to scan an arc of 180 degrees or more on each side of the body. To the fish's rear there is a small blind spot where neither eye can see. Dead ahead, the arcs of the two eyes overlap to provide a narrow band—perhaps 45 degrees— where the fish has binocular, or stereoscopic, vision. It is in this band of binocular vision that a fish can be expected to have accurate depth perception. But sharpness of vision is lost in the tradeoff because the image is focused out near the periphery of the retina. The sharpest vision would occur when objects are at a right angle to the eye.

In chasing down prey or a lure where depth perception is important, a fish would attack straight ahead. This straight-on position gives a fish the maximum ability to estimate target distance. At the same time, certain fish—billfish are an example—do try to get a better look at their quarry by swinging from side to side. This may be because their frontal vision is obscured by their bill, but the zigzag approach also places the prey closer to a right angle to the eye where vision is sharpest.

If you've ever watched a trout on its feeding station, you've probably noticed the fish turn right or left occasionally. This serves one of two purposes. Either the fish is turning at a right angle to suspected prey, to get a better look, or turning to bring the prey into the zone of binocular vision where depth perception is possible. Possibly the trout is alternating the two techniques for maximum advantage. Without depth perception a fish has a hard time getting the range of its target and hitting the mark.

In presenting a bait or lure to a fish that you can see underwater the natural tendency is to sweep the offering in front of the fish because that's where humans see best. There are even some anglers who insist on putting the bait or lure right in front of the fish's nose. In light of the way a fish sees, this may

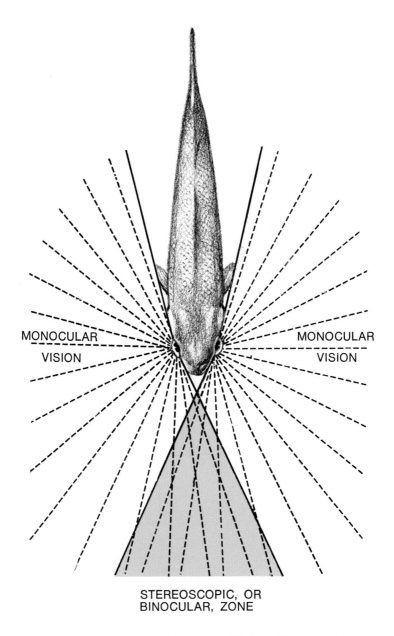

MONOCULAR

VISION

MONOCULAR

VISION

STEREOSCOPIC, OR
BINOCULAR, ZONE

Owing to the placement of their eyes, fish have binocular vision only
in a small area in front of them. Each eye, however, can scan an arc of
180 degrees to the side. Eye placement is shown very well in the
head-on photo of the rock bass at right.

or may not be a good approach. Although most of the super
predators see well dead ahead, some fish do not. Anglers
fishing for sharks in clear, shallow water, for example, know
that a shark has particularly poor vision. Therefore, they
place the lure at right angles to the fish's eye. Anglers fishing
for tarpon, bonefish, or dozens of other species advocate placing the lure in front of the fish, making it easier for it to ingest
the offering without changing direction. Nevertheless, there's
still much to be said for placing the lure alongside the fish's
eye. The fish may have to turn to bring the lure into binocular focus, but the line won't be moving across the water in
front of him.

HOW FISH REACT TO MOVEMENT

In the fish's world, where the water is usually murky and the light flat, objects tend to blend with background. For that reason, fish are very quick to discern movement and contrast. A stationary object may go unseen, but add a bit of motion and fish will react immediately. Perhaps they sense danger or possibly the presence of food.

Cast a small topwater popper on the surface of a bluegill pond and chances are that a school will move in to examine the intruder. Sometimes a bluegill will strike the lure as it lies still on the water, but usually they'll all line up a few inches to a couple of feet away and watch. The instant you move the popper, a bluegill has it. That little bit of motion triggered the response.

Not long ago, we had the pleasure of being with Art Flick, an expert trout fisherman, on a small stream in New York State. It was late summer, the fast water was gone, and a dry spell made you wonder whether there could possibly be trout in that brook. The stream had pretty well settled into still pockets that held fish. Art's dry fly hung limply on the sur-face—as unappetizing a morsel as any fish could imagine. To improve things, he imparted motion to the fly by twitching it on the surface. That fly hadn't moved 2 feet when a 15-inch rainbow sucked it under the surface. On the next cast, another trout had it. Art had a picnic taking and releasing nice trout all afternoon in water that looked barren—all by giving the fly a little motion.

Almost any predatory fish will examine anything moving through its field of vision. Fish are curious creatures. Scientists have discovered that fish become excited to some degree when they see movement. Experiments were conducted by shining a microscopic beam of light through the lens of a fish's eye at various angles. By studying the retina, scientists found that the slightest movement of the beam excites the nerves and is relayed to the brain instantly. Thus the retina constantly signals the movement of objects via the nervous system to the action center that stimulates the fish's interest.

CONTRAST AND SHADE

Research with the beam scanner and basic anatomy studies have also demonstrated that fish are visually alert to contrast. Any object that contrasts with its surroundings in color, light value, or brightness is sensed quickly by the fish and provokes its curiosity. The problem every fisherman faces is carrying the motivation of the fish from the curiosity stage to one of excitement and attack. There certainly is no clear-cut answer to this problem, but combining contrast with movement should be promising.

If you're fishing artificials, don't stop the retrieve. Once you do, you can expect the fish to realize the offering is unnatural and to stop following. Speed it up, pause for an instant, and then speed it up again. If that doesn't work, try a different approach and keep changing until you do get a strike. Some anglers try to provoke a fish by taking the lure away. They reason that they don't want the fish to get a good look at the lure and reject it permanently. But considering the turbidity of the water, the nearsightedness of fish, and the fact that the lure is moving, a fish seldom has time to study a lure carefully. After all, the "prey" is trying to escape. There is something about its behavior or appearance that makes a gamefish think it's a meal. It could be just a flash or a contrasting color that is moving. Perhaps it's the undulation or a combination of factors. Whatever it is, it triggers a response in the fish.

Although color patterns of artificial lures can be important under certain conditions, they are seldom as critical as anglers believe them to be. If you're not having success with an artificial and have fished it diligently, varying the retrieve and the presentation, then the first step is to switch to a lure of a different size. If you know what the fish are feeding on, try to approximate the size. If you don't know, try lures of varying size. Size is generally much more significant to a fish than color. At the same time, you could be varying the shape or silhouette along with the size.

Doug Swisher, an experienced Michigan fly fisherman, has

made a study of insects on which trout feed and come up with the fact that the average size of an insect in the waters he fishes is only 7.2 millimeters (less than one-third of an inch). Translated to the language of the fisherman, this represents a normal tie on a No. 16 hook. Doug catches most of his trout on flies smaller than a No. 16 and actually ties some down to No. 28.

After carefully studying the insect hatches in Michigan for a number of years, Swisher decided that the silhouette was the most important aspect when it corresponded to size. His duns have the wings perfectly upright and he doesn't use hackle to make the flies float. Instead, he relies on a fur body and a pair of stabilizers near the tail to keep the offering upright. He claims he does equally well on any fly that approximates the size and silhouette of the hatch. He will fish a light fly or a dark one depending on the basic coloration of the hatch. Having fished with Doug, we've seen his methods work to perfection.

THE MIRROR EFFECT

Fish are constantly adjusting to changes in light. Most of the changes of light underwater are not sudden, but gradual shadings of illumination from day to night, surface to bottom, clear to turbid, and so forth. Light is usually scattered and dispersed in water, making for these subtle changes. But at the surface where the change from water to air is abrupt, the change in light is also abrupt. When light enters the water at the surface, it is bent strongly by refraction, bounced around, broken up by ripples on the water, and much of it reflected back to the sky. All of these factors have important and sometimes remarkable effects on the vision of fish.

When the surface of a lake or estuary is glassy calm, its underside is a partial mirror. A fish looking up into this mirror can not only see what is in the water above, but also anything moving about below. If the water is shallow as well as calm, the fish can see a good bit of the bottom and thereby detect any creature lurking on the far side of a rock or log that cannot be seen directly.

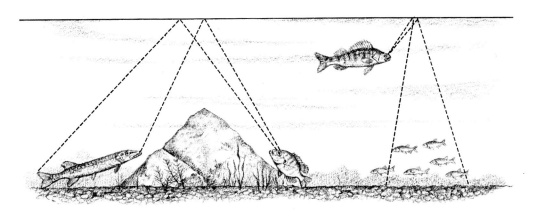

When a lake is perfectly calm on the surface, a mirror is created
which reflects large areas of the bottom. Fish can see in this mirror
reflections of predators or prey they could not see directly *(above)*.
In the photo below, a glassy surface has become a perfect mirror
for the sunfish in the foreground.

When you cast on a calm day, and your line settles on the surface, to the fish below it is seen as a long crack in their mirror or even as a shadow across the bottom that is reflected in the mirror. Once a fish is alerted by any movement in the mirror, its total attention is focused on the invading object until its fears are put to rest. It is on the alert and much more difficult to fool.

If you're fishing under such conditions, there are several things you can do to minimize the disadvantage. If you're fly fishing, try a longer and finer leader. Some experts switch to leaders that are 12 or 14 feet long, reducing the amount of heavier line in the water to make that crack in the mirror appear less obvious. Another important consideration is to present your lure much farther from the fish, and then, after the lure sinks, work it into his range of underwater vision. At times, smaller lures are dictated because they create less of a shadow as they cross the water during the cast. If you are experimentally minded, put on a diving mask and pretend you're a fish while a friend casts over you. This can be done in a swimming pool and the lesson will be indelibly imprinted in your mind.

THE PERISCOPE EFFECT

Most fishermen realize that a fish can also look *through* the partial mirror at the surface—particularly if it is relatively calm—and see what's above the water. The scene includes you or your tackle if you happen to be standing at the edge of a pond or in a boat. When you are in view, the slightest movement you make can frighten your quarry away. The fish has the advantage since the light rays reflecting off your body are bent downward by refraction when they enter the surface of the water. This gives the fish a sort of periscopic view of things. The effect depends on the angle at which the fish is looking out. Bending of light increases with the flatness of view. As an example, a fish looking upward at an angle of 42 degrees will see light rays entering the water at an angle of 10 degrees. Light striking the water at less than 10 degrees is reflected away without reaching the fish's eye. In fact, light penetration is really poor until an angle of 20 degrees is reached, meaning that a fish would need a bright day with clear water to see much of whatever was on the shore below an angle of 20 degrees.

Very often, the angler is hidden below the 20-degree angle, but his rod waves well above it during the cast. And the movement of the rod is enough to send a fish streaking for cover. Anglers are sometimes puzzled in the shallow, clear

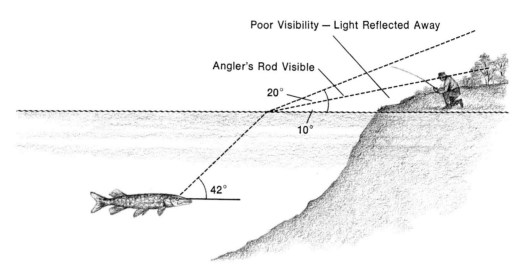

Fish can see a fisherman on the bank because water refracts light waves. In the diagram, a fish looking upward at an angle of 42 degrees would see light rays entering the water at 10 degrees—that is, it would see the fisherman's rod, of if he stood up, his body. Below 10 degrees, light is reflected *off* the water and the fish couldn't see well. Naturally, it pays to stay low on the bank of a lake or river.

flats of the Florida Keys when a school of fish starts to spook before the line ever touches the water. One reason is that the rod tip and the line are often visible while moving through the air. Recently, flylines are being manufactured in a dull gray finish that minimizes contrast, making it harder for the fish to spot line movement.

That same afternoon that Art Flick was giving his dry fly motion he demonstrated a strategy that more trout fishermen should follow. Walking back away from the edge of the stream, Art located a promising pool in which he wanted to start and, dropping on his hands and knees, crawled commando-style until he was in position to cast. Trout fishermen too often make the mistake of walking right up to the stream bank when the water is shallow and clear. If they do see fish, the fish are usually streaking across the stream bed for another safer lie. To the uninitiated, an angler approaching a stream like a commando may be a ridiculous sight. Yet, when the day is over and the creels inspected, the angler who took precautionary measures is usually way ahead.

CAN FISH SEE COLOR?

The aspect of fish vision that has been questioned more than any other is whether or not fish can see color. To the angler who relies on artificial lures, this question is of paramount importance.

From a scientific standpoint, there is one definite answer to the question of color and that is a very emphatic *yes*. Fish can and do see color. Some species can distinguish colors better than others, but nearly all of them do see color. However, there is more to the story.

Colors correspond to the various wavelengths of light energy emanating from an object. Radiant energy is called "light" when it is of the proper wavelengths to stimulate the optical nerves in the retina of the eye. The waves with which we are concerned range in length from 1/33,000 to 1/67,000 of an inch. Light falling within this range is in the visible spectrum. Ultraviolet and infrared light are both outside of the visible spectrum and cannot be seen by the eye.

The color of light varies by shadings starting with blues at the end of the spectrum where the waves are shortest. These are followed by greens, yellows, and oranges, until red is reached at the longer end of the spectrum. White light is made up of all the colors or wave lengths mixed together. Thus, when you see an object of a specific color, you are seeing only that one part of the color spectrum of natural light that is reflected back to you. The rest of the wavelengths have been absorbed into the object and removed from the spectrum.

We are all familiar with seeing color through the medium of air, but other changes take place when the medium is a fluid. Water absorbs the radiant energy of light as heat, altering it rapidly as it passes through the depths. It's really a filtering process in which certain wave lengths are selectively removed at specific depths. This changes the composition of the spectrum and alters the color characteristics of light.

Color is absorbed from the light as it passes through the water toward the object and then again when it is reflected from the object and passes back from the object to your eye through the medium of water. Since the wavelengths reaching your eye determine the color that the object appears to you, a lure seen from above the surface will have lost a great deal of color because of the double passage of light rays through the water. A fish at a particular depth, however, is concerned with only the light loss from the surface to that depth, and for a short distance through the water to its eyes.

As you go deeper a body of water becomes darker and darker because the light rays are absorbed and the particles in the water scatter the light. Some of the light, of course, is reflected back toward the surface. Water absorbs the longer waves (the reds) fastest. The shorter waves, blues and greens, are absorbed slowest. Therefore, the deeper one goes, the less red and the more blue and green there is in the remaining light. Red light disappears so rapidly that even in clear water it is almost all gone at a depth of 20 or 30 feet. In typical murky water, red light is gone even sooner. As the warm colors rapidly give way to the cool colors, the fish's world takes on a monotonous blue-green aspect.

The color vision of fish is generally comparable to that of humans. Therefore we can assume that a fish detects the same striking changes in apparent color as does a skin diver descending into the depths. With the near absence of red light below 15 or 20 feet, a plug that appeared pure red at the surface would appear black. If the plug were not true red, but interspersed with green and blue pigments, it would take on a dark greenish-gray or blue appearance.

Because yellow is made up of shorter wavelengths that penetrate the water more easily, a yellow object will retain its original color to a much greater depth than a red one. Consequently, a yellow plug would still look yellow considerably below 20 feet, but the color would not be nearly as bright as it is at the surface. A blue or green plug would hold close to its original color regardless of how deep it was fished. But in very deep water where the whole aspect is blue-green, a blue or green plug would not show up very well against the same colored background.

To put the idea of color extinction in relation to depth in useful form, we have calculated the percentage of penetration of light for different colors. These values are for very clear water and represent the maximum penetration. Naturally, this penetration would be greatly reduced as the clarity of the water diminishes. The table shows how red is almost nonexistent near the surface. In the clearest water, only 1/40 of 1 percent of true red light remains at 30 feet.

On the other hand, 69 percent of green light remains at the same depth. It is surprising that orange light, which is very close to red in the spectrum, penetrates so well. The 12 percent of orange remaining at 30 feet (in very clear water) is more than adequate for good visibility of orange objects even at dawn or dusk.

LIGHT PENETRATION DEPTHS

Color	10 Feet	20 Feet	30 Feet
Red	6.5%	0.4%	0.025%
Orange	50%	25%	12%
Yellow	73%	53%	40%
Green	88%	78%	69%

Note: These color penetrations will be greatly reduced in turbid water depending on the amount and type of particles.

At dusk, when the underwater light begins to fall rapidly below the fish's threshold of color vision, the reds are the first to go, followed by orange, yellow, and finally green and blue. When the total light level falls below one foot-candle, the fish have switched to sensitive rod vision and are unable to discern color, even in bright moonlight.

At dawn, the pattern is reversed when the fish switch to color-sensitive cone vision. Blue and green are the first colors visible in the early-morning light, followed by the warmer colors. Basically, in low light levels, the major concern of the angler should be whether to use lures that are dark or light. Fish may distinguish shadings, but in most circumstances, the distinction of light value is all that is necessary.

Years back, we fished the Susquehanna River quite regularly near the point where it empties into Chesapeake Bay. The target was largemouth bass and striped bass. Both fish often ranged the same territory and the best fishing seemed to be in the late afternoon until dark. They were gluttons for a surface plug, and although a variety of models and colors worked from tea time to the normal supper hour, you had to switch to a dark plug (preferably black) at dusk. It becomes apparent now (although we weren't aware of it then) that the sky remained light in color long after the surrounding territory began to get dark, and the black plug was clearly visible to the fish against the light background.

We have talked about color vision in fish as though all species can see equally well and discern color with equal ability. This is an oversimplification, of course. While most species appear to have color vision to a degree, some are much sharper at color discrimination than others. Anatomists, familiar with vision of animals, know that the presence of cone sensors in the retina indicates a basic capability for color vision. Since nearly all fish have cones, the assumption is that they are all color sensitive to a degree. Sharks are an exception because they have only black and white rod sensors. Snappers living on the bottom in the subtropics are another exception. A deep-water fish like the snapper would have little use for red sensitivity, since it lives where there is no red light.

Among the various fresh- and saltwater gamefishes, the shallow-water species appear to have highly developed color vision, probably equal to ours. They have good perception over a wide range of the color spectrum from the long-wave reds to the short-wave blues. Experiments have proved that certain shallow-water fishes can discriminate between *twenty-four different color hues*—delicate shadings of color from the blue end to the red end of the spectrum. It is certainly logical that shallow-water fish would have the best color vision because they live near the surface where there is light ranging through the whole spectrum.

A particularly interesting study conducted a number of years ago demonstrated conclusively that the largemouth bass responded to red above all colors. Further work confirmed this and added that violet closely approximated red to the fish. Green is probably the color that a bass sees second best. Yellow and blue appear less distinct and almost identical with black. The experimenters concluded that a largemouth is relatively yellow-blue blind—at least, it doesn't react to those colors.

Surprisingly, it was proven that bass can see colors above the surface of the water and could respond to that color before it reached the water. The same study demonstrated that a bass has difficulty separating yellow from light gray, blue from dark gray or black, but can easily distinguish intensity.

In spite of this research, we also know that largemouth bass are taken regularly on lures of almost every color. The fact that they can discriminate some colors better than others is no guarantee that they won't strike the other colors. Movement of the lure is a major factor and the related noise of a surface lure is another. Yet, knowing this color preference, you may want to do some experimenting of your own.

Nature has provided many baitfish species with protective coloration. Over the years, fishermen have always tried to duplicate the color and shape of bait when buying or making artificial lures. On the other hand, it is interesting to speculate what might happen if fishermen used lures that were highly visible, even though they bore no resemblance in color pattern to anything a fish had ever seen before. This is being done to some extent with fluorescent colors and at times these lures work well. Yet, there is no concrete evidence that a fish responds better to a brightly colored imitation.

Experienced saltwater fishermen who use leadheaded bucktail jigs in water depths from 60 to 180 feet invariably favor white. The standard jig has shiny mylar interspersed through the white bucktail for higher visibility. Occasionally, someone will try a blue jig (which also retains its color in the depths), but white is still the number one choice.

Some anglers argue that contrast among the colors is important and this may very well be true. Unfortunately, scientific evidence to either support or refute this opinion is not available. It makes sense, however, to offer the fish something it can see.

At Ridge Lake, George Bennett found that the most successful casters used red and white plugs, confirming the research conclusions of F. A. Brown that "... red appears to be the outstanding color, as such, in the responses of bass. This color is easily and readily selected from everything else, with the exception of violet." Dr. Brown listed yellow as a close second best in getting a response from bass. To confirm this, Ridge Lake fly fishermen got their top bass catches on yellow or yellow and white streamers—even though other evidence would indicate bass cannot tell yellow from gray or white!

Gamefish have different abilities in discerning the color of prey or lures. From an extensive series of tests with lures of various colors in fresh water, Elgin Ciampi rated the color vision of the largemouth bass as being the best. This was followed in order by smallmouth bass, muskie, northern pike, rainbow trout, bluegill, crappie, and gar. Again we find that the versatile largemouth heads the list.

If you remember nothing more about fish vision than how a fish sees your offering before the strike, you've gained an edge. Sound or smell might lead it to your bait, but the final attack is dictated by sight in almost every instance. Therefore, if you can get a bait or lure in front of the fish in a natural manner and it is approximately the correct size and shape (and possibly color), you should score well.

4

The
Sense
of
Smell

Fish live a mysterious existence in a shadowy world, a world in which they cannot depend on sight alone. To monitor their surroundings, they must rely on the skillful use of all five senses. Since we humans also possess the senses of sight, smell, hearing, taste, and touch, we tend to assume that fish perceive and respond just as we do.

Fishermen are frequently guilty of what scientists call anthropomorphism. It's nothing more serious than attributing human characteristics to animals. Both fish and man need food, cover, and protection from their enemies for survival. But the ways of life and the habitats of fish differ greatly from those of man. That's why you can't always figure out what you would do in a given situation if you were a fish and then expect the fish to exhibit the anticipated response.

It's easier to understand fish if you learn how they are motivated. The sense of smell is a prime example. If we fall victim to anthropomorphic thinking, it would be easy to discount the importance of smell, because our own sense of smell is not really acute. A fish, on the other hand, has a highly developed olfactory sense that is extremely complex, forming the largest part of a fish's brain. That alone is enough to tell us that the sense of smell is essential to a fish's survival.

ANATOMY OF SMELL

Science has discovered many fascinating and useful facts about the sense of smell in fishes, demonstrating that certain species can scent food or danger with incredible sensitivity. As a general rule, you can assume that if a fish species prefers muddy or turbid water or if it shows a preference for feeding at night, it has a highly developed sense of smell. And fish that boast a keen sense of smell are usually easier to take on natural bait than they are on artificials. Smell will lead them a long distance toward the bait under conditions of poor visibility.

Fish can sense a far greater range of odor-producing chemicals in the water than we can in the air. The salmon is the textbook example. Salmon navigate hundreds even thousands of miles, using smell to seek out the river of their birth for spawning. But even the smallest minnow puts its olfactory sense to good use, and there are some baitfish that will panic at the scent of a wounded schoolmate.

Like any air-breathing animal, a fish has two nostrils in its snout. Each nostril leads to a separate olfactory organ. Unlike air breathers, however, the fish's nostrils don't connect with the throat. Instead, they each end in a shallow chamber lined with a sensory pad of epithelium so highly developed for detecting odors that it contains a half million olfactory cells for each square inch of its surface.

Good odor perception requires that water from the fish's surroundings be moved rapidly over these olfactory cells.

Nostrils on this largemouth bass are clearly visible. Each one leads to an ultra-sensitive olfactory organ. Thousands of tiny, hairlike structures, pulsing in sequence, force water through the nostrils and into the olfactory chamber.

Therefore, fish that hunt by smell have an arrangement to circulate the water rapidly over the organ. Thousands of tiny, hairlike structures (called cilia) pulse in sequence, forcing the water down through the chamber. Some species supplement this pumping arrangement by contracting and expanding a portion of the nasal chamber each time the gill covers are moved for breathing. The principle is similar to that of the human lung.

Species with two nostrils on each side of the snout are the ones with a potential for excellent odor perception, because water can pass into the chamber through the front nostril and out the back one. This results in a fast, clean flow of water over the sensory pads. If a fish has only a single nostril on each side of the snout leading to the chamber, you can assume that the sense of smell is not as keen as in other species and probably isn't critical in finding food.

Most gamefish species have the double nostril system or a

modification in which the sensing organ is covered by a simple flap of skin with an inlet in front and an outlet at the rear. But unless they have either the cilia or pumping systems to force water through the chamber, they will still lack sophisticated odor perception when they are at rest. Consequently, they must either swim continuously or station themselves in a current to benefit from the flow of water. In some species, the front nostril curves up and flares out to form a scoop which points forward and deflects the flow of water through the chamber while the fish is swimming.

The arrangement of nostrils and the system of forcing water through them give us a major clue to the ability of a species to smell. Fish anatomists, however, find further clues to the olfactory perception inside the fish's head. The olfactory sense center is in the forebrain (telencephalon or paleo cortex) and consists of right and left lobes. Large nerves connect each brain lobe to an olfactory bulb between the brain and the nostril. The bulb, in turn, connects via a nerve trunk to the pad of sensors in the nasal chamber. Fish with keen odor perception have large olfactory bulbs and large forebrains. The highly developed smell system is particularly characteristic of bottom-dwelling species that exist where light levels are low. Since the bottom dwellers normally feed by smelling out their prey, natural bait would have to be the primary choice for angling.

SMELL VS. SIGHT

Dr. H. Kleerekoper, an expert on fish senses, notes that smell can work in two ways. Often, the sense of smell creates an awareness in the fish that food is somewhere about. Once this determination is made by the fish, it switches to vision for the actual location of the prey. But when there is a flow of water—a current or tide to carry the odor in a definite direction from the source—the fish may continue to track by smell.

Scientists have run a number of experiments on different species of fish in which they plugged the nostrils and then offered food. In the scientists' tanks most species could locate the food visually, but freshwater catfish, eels, and some sharks were totally helpless. Gamefish are primarily visual feeders and sight is usually the key sense. However, smell may play a vital role as an advance or long-range detector. At middle ranges from their prey, hearing becomes an important adjunct. Thus a fish can track down its quarry through a combination of smell and sound until close enough to spot it visually.

The yellow perch is a freshwater species with a sharp sense of smell. In the briny, the codfish is a classic representative of oceanic bottom fishes that have good noses for living in the dim depths of the sea. Then there's the striped bass, a truly versatile species that often feeds aggressively at night. Finding a black eel on a black night isn't easy unless the predator has a keen nose. Acute odor perception is an asset to the channel bass while plying its trade in murky water with low visibility. Called redfish in Florida and along the Gulf Coast, the channel bass is notoriously nearsighted. It will strike an artificial lure only if it's placed right in front of him; but otherwise reds rely on their sense of smell to locate food. The fierce moray eel hides by day in caves or holes among the rocks or coral reefs, hunting at night with its nose. And at the extreme in fresh water, there are cave-dwelling species that are totally blind, feeding only by smell and taste.

Results from a series of experiments on the sense of smell show that the least honors for odor perception should go to the northern pike. Most fish species tested detected the presence of food from its odor and readily tracked it down, no matter where it was put in the tank. But the pike just swam around ignoring the food unless it was put right out in the open where it could be seen. Although equipped with a poor sense of smell, the northern has few equals when it comes to vision. Any baitfish that comes into range of the pike's keen eyes is a goner. Yet at night, the northern is generally helpless and must spend the hours of darkness resting and biding its time. Most fish that do not feed at night are true sight feeders. The traditional dark-of-night feeders rely on their sense of smell.

Some species are hard to categorize as specialists in any

one of the senses. The black basses are true generalists. They have sharp vision combined with an excellent sense of smell and first-rate hearing. Consequently, they feed under a variety of conditions and hit well on both live bait and artificials.

The practice of dropping leadheaded bucktails to the bottom and working them toward the surface is a deadly fishing technique when the sun is high and the visibility is good. At the low light levels of early morning or late afternoon bucktail jigs are not nearly as effective, nor are they so potent in the dim light of 120 feet to 180 feet of water. But if you hang a strip of bait or a whole balao on the jig hook, the number of strikes will increase as the fish are stimulated by smell.

In an experiment off the deeper reefs near Walker's Cay in the Bahamas, we fished a leadheaded bucktail (deep jig) side by side with two anglers fishing natural bait. It was late in the afternoon and light levels were low. The artificial wouldn't produce a fish, while the natural bait constantly found the action. When the jig was baited, the picture changed and it started to take fish. Smell had to be the factor that brought the fish within visual range of the offering. So

Odor of live bait on a teaser rig attracts a cobia to the surface, the commotion attracting an entire school. Often when artificial lures fail to bring a strike, live bait will by arousing a fish's sense of smell.

unless you're adamant about using only artificial lures for deep jigging, experiment with a strip of bait on the jig hook and you'll see the difference.

HOW CHUM WORKS

The whole theory of chumming is based on the ability of fish to track prey through the sense of smell. It really makes little difference whether the chummer is tossing kernels of corn, shrimp, clams, conch, or ground fish in the water. The idea is to get the fish to follow up against the flow until they reach the source of the chum. Therefore, to chum properly, a current or tide should be running, carrying the scent to the fish. Saltwater chummers frequently notice that fishing drops off considerably when the tide slackens, picking up again as the tide starts to run. If you're chumming in a freshwater stream with corn or salmon eggs, you don't face the problem because the current is always flowing.

Chumming is also an effective technique near a reef or coral head. The trick is to anchor up current and let the chum drift back to where the fish should be. Ground-up fish makes an excellent chumline and this can be sweetened by tossing whole pilchards or other small baitfish overboard.

There are several theories on chumming that are worthy of consideration. Any angler who has chummed bluefish in the Northeast can tell you that within a minute or two after the chumline stops, the fish move off. Therefore, it is most important to keep the slick going at an even pace. A good rule of thumb is to dump another ladle over as the previous one begins to disappear from sight. And the rule of continuous chumming holds even while you are fighting a fish. Otherwise, you'll lose the school and have to work to get them back.

Some specialists believe you should chum heavily until you get fish behind the boat and then resort to a watered-down solution to keep the fish there. Your mission is to attract fish and not to feed them. Don't keep ladling gobs and gobs of chum; instead, taper the chumline to bring the fish to the boat.

Experience has shown that oily fish make a better ground chum because the odor carries much farther and the oil causes a slick on the surface of the water. Even cans of sardines mashed with bread or oatmeal can be used for chum. You can also use catfood made from a fish base.

To bring fish up from deep water, mix the chum with sand and then toss it over. The sand helps to carry the scent into the depths. Small, white pebbles embedded in the chum will serve the same purpose. The idea is to get the aroma of the free meal over as wide a stretch of water as possible.

There are many ways of fishing in a chumline. In some situations, the approved technique is to wait until specific fish are sighted and then cast to them or present a bait. In other types of chumming, like bluefish chumming, the best method is to drift a natural bait back with the chum. Keep in mind that the fish are accustomed to picking up free-floating tidbits and your bait should follow the slick in a natural manner. That means that you should keep free-spooling line so the bait on your hook keeps pace with the slick at the exact rate of drift.

This same technique has been used effectively by flyrod fishermen while working a chumslick. All they do is cast a fly into the slick and strip extra line in the water so that the fly settles naturally. Gamefish will grab the fly even though it is seemingly dead in the water, since they have been feeding on free-floating chunks of bait. For this purpose, a relatively shiny fly that resembles the baitfish will work well.

When you're swimming a bait or fly in a chumslick, keep your eye on the loose line coiled on the water's surface. That will provide the first indication of a strike. Under normal conditions, the line will move away from you at a steady pace, carried by the tide or current. But the instant it starts to tighten at a faster rate, you know a fish has picked up the bait. Make sure your reel is in gear and push the rod toward the line as it straightens. This is called "shotgunning" and it gives the fish an extra instant to ingest the bait. As you feel the strain of the strike, lift the rod tip sharply to set the hook. When fish first enter a chumslick, they might take the bait in their mouth very gingerly, taste-testing it before clamping down. If you were to set the hook too soon, you could pull the bait right out of a fish's mouth. That's why shotgunning is a favored technique when the fish aren't hitting with authority. It provides a little extra time before the fish realizes that something is wrong.

If you're not getting strikes by swimming a bait in the slick near the surface, try adding a small sinker to take it deeper. Fish don't always follow the accepted pattern and there are times when they will hang well back in a chumslick, refusing to come any closer to the boat. That's why it pays to float a line way back behind the boat before bringing it in to start again. And you'll also find that lighter lines coupled with small hooks and tiny pieces of bait are more apt to follow the course of a slick when the current is erratic.

Chumming is just as effective in fresh water although it is not practiced very much. Fly fishermen using terrestrials often toss natural insects into the stream to put the fish in a feeding mood and also to locate specific lies. Salmon eggs tossed into a stream also work well and trout sometimes will work upstream following them to their source. You can do the same thing with corn, cheese, and other strongly scented baits.

SENSITIVITY OF SMELL

Although scientists have mapped out the olfactory system rather completely, they still don't know exactly how fish are able to discern and discriminate between thousands of odors. One theory holds that some type of enzyme action takes place. We do know that an electric signal is sent through a nerve fiber to the brain when an odor is detected. And we also know that the response is much higher in a hungry fish than in one that has recently fed. Experiments show that the signal is again higher when a fish first senses the odor than after a period of exposure to it.

But the experts are baffled by the extreme sensitivity of smell in fishes. Fish can react to smaller traces of chemicals in the water than most scientific instruments can detect. For example, sockeye salmon can sense an extract of shrimp in the water when it is present at only one part to 100 million parts of water—equivalent to a third of a teaspoon (12 drops) in a large swimming pool (23,000 gallons.)

Salmon are equally gifted in the ability to smell out their enemies. Both coho (silver salmon) and chinooks (king salmon) can detect incredibly light odors from seals and sea lions, their natural enemies. Experiments showed them able to detect extracts of seal or sea lion skin at dilutions of one part per 80 billion—less than two hundreths of a drop in that same 23,000 gallon swimming pool!

Further tests demonstrated that salmon swimming through fish ladders on spawning runs turned tail and ran back downstream when a man rinsed his hands in the water some distance upstream. However, the same migrating salmon were not affected by dozens of other substances tested, including tomato juice and even urine. It makes you wonder about touching baits or simply putting your hand in the water. Salmon are frightened by odors given off by man, seals, and bears. The actual substance in the skin surface of mammals that is detected by fish is called L-serine.

The all-out champion of underwater smell is the American eel. A set of remarkable experiments showed that this species of fish can sense a certain alcohol (B-Phenyl ethyl) at test dilutions equal to less than one billionth of a drop in a large swimming pool. At this degree of sensitivity, an eel needs just a single molecule within its nostril to detect the presence of alcohol. This super-keen olfactory ability is related to their habit of living and feeding around muddy bottoms where visibility is near zero and eyesight is of little use. It also serves them well in their juvenile migration from the Sargasso Sea south of Bermuda to coastal streams thousands of miles away along the Atlantic shoreline. And it's mainly done by sense of smell.

On several trips, we have experimented with a bluegill's sense of smell and his caution when human odors are present. Normally, in tying on a small fly you have to touch it. Or you've handled the fly when removing it from the mouth of a fish. Sometimes when this happens, the bluegills will refuse to take the fly until about the fifth or sixth cast—just long enough for some of the odor to dissipate. If you find yourself in that situation, pop the fly into your mouth (being careful of course to avoid the hook) and wet it with saliva. Then, without touching the fly, make a cast. The bluegills will strike it avidly.

SHARKS AND SMELL

Perhaps the best example of a species that relies on smell as its main sense for finding food is the shark. Some sharks have an olfactory apparatus so developed that it occupies two-thirds of their entire brain. The eyesight of most sharks is unquestionably poor and they compensate for this by using smell and sound (vibrations in the water) to locate food. One exception is the mako shark, which has rather good eyesight and feeds visually. The mako will hit an artificial lure readily if it is presented correctly. The black-tip shark also has better than average vision for a shark and can be taken on an artificial lure. Many sharks will strike a lure if they can find it, but their vision is poor and the lure has to be placed near their eye.

Sharks combine their extreme sensitivity to smell with a rapid and accurate directional ability. They often swim a zig-zag rather than a straight course. The instant a shark senses an odor, it begins a search pattern, zigging left when the odor is stronger in the left nostril and zagging right when the odor is stronger in the right nostril. This leads the shark to the source of the odor rapidly where he hopes to find a wounded fish that will make an easy meal.

Blood in the water is particularly attractive to sharks. Small quantities of fish blood often have drained out of a fish box through scuppers and have attracted sharks. One such occurrence off the New Jersey coast brought a pair of sharks that promptly tried to sink their teeth into the transom of a 31-foot boat. They were trying to get at the source of the blood, and since both sharks were more than 19 feet long, the anglers tossed the fish overboard and fired up the engines.

A similar event occurred while we were fishing off Grand Cay in the Bahamas in a 17-foot skiff. We had a single fish in the well that we had promised to one of the local families and were drifting over an offshore reef when a 6-foot hammerhead shark appeared. He promptly rammed the transom of the skiff and we realized instantly that blood from our catch had oozed into the water, attracting the shark. Immediately, we started the outboard and ran at a good clip for some distance. Five minutes after we shut down the engine, the same shark was back with us. We didn't waste a minute in starting the engine and we ran a good fifteen minutes in another direction. The shark never showed again.

SPECIAL SMELLS

Many fishes respond in fright to the smell of a wounded member of their own species. Experiments on this effect started when behavioral scientist Dr. von Frisch noticed that if a bird dropped a wounded baitfish back into the water, the school fled the spot and avoided a wide area surrounding it for a long time afterwards. Von Frisch's subsequent laboratory experiments demonstrated that fish are remarkably sensitive to tiny amounts of a substance from the skin of wounded schoolmates. When a pike, for example, attacks a single minnow, enough alarm substance is given off by the prey to start an escape panic among the rest of the minnows, a delayed response which takes place about thirty seconds later. Any system based on smell cannot give instant warning of attack (like vision can) because of the time required for diffusion and reaction. But the odor alarm lingers in an area and minnows can gain a good deal of protection by knowing that they should avoid a general area where a predator has been foraging around and attacking other baitfish.

The alarm substance the minnows react to is called *schreckstoff*. It is easily visible by microscope in certain cells of their skin tissue. Muscle tissue also contains smaller amounts of *schreckstoff*, but it is not found in the intestines. The fright reaction of the minnows has been proven to be instinctual, rather than learned, because in experiments fish panicked that had never smelled *schreckstoff* in water before. To prove that the sense of smell was involved, scientists blocked the nostrils of other experimental fish and no panic reaction was evident.

There are numerous other examples of how smell helps small baitfish protect themselves. Experiments with a European minnow have demonstrated another type of fright behavior. When the odor of a pike was added to a tank full of these minnows, the minnows reacted by either freezing in place immediately or by rushing around in panic and then going to the bottom to freeze in place. They seemed to know that pike are sight feeders, preferring to strike moving targets primarily, and that it is safest to remain motionless. More remarkable is the fact that this is a learned behavior gained from experience and it is not instinctual like the response to *schreckstoff*. Minnows that had never been threatened by a pike did not react to the smell of a pike.

When pike attack mosquito fish (another bait species), the prey flees toward the surface, often jumping clear of the water. Mosquito fish, like some of the other minnow species, detect the odor of pike in the water and they respond by panicking. If water containing pike odor is added to their tank, they rush toward the surface and jump out or otherwise follow the escape procedure they normally would if a real pike were attacking.

In further experiments, it has been discovered that fish can use the olfactory system to recognize others of their own species as well as close relatives. One scientist reports that a minnow could be trained to recognize any of fifteen other closely related minnow-like species. Moreover, he claims that a fish can even identify one individual fish of its own species from all others just by smell. There are certainly enough examples of the remarkable olfactory sensitivity in fish to clearly indicate that no angler can afford to overlook it in planning his fishing strategy.

The sense of smell in fish is not limited to food alone. Their talent for sniffing encompasses a wide variety of natural substances and they can easily detect the odors of a full range of aquatic plants and even soil that is washed into the water. The bluntnose minnow, for example, can find its way home if it gets lost by following specific plant odors. Sunfish can also perform the same feat.

NAVIGATION BY SMELL

When it comes to navigating by the sense of smell, the salmons lead the field. Their precision is incredible. The young are born in gravel beds of small tributaries often hundreds of miles from bay or ocean. After hatching, the juvenile fish stay close to their birth spot for a year or so, feeding, gaining strength, and becoming thoroughly familiar with the exact combination of smells that occur on their particular home-ground. Scientists would say that the smells are "imprinted" in the brain of the fish.

At a point in their life cycle, the salmon move toward the ocean (or Great Lakes in the case of the cohos and chinooks that were transplanted), migrating hundreds and even thousands of miles in the process. In the ocean, the salmon feed voraciously and fatten over a period of another year or two. Then, they start the journey home, returning to spawn on the exact spot where they were born. They retrace their path over the hundreds or thousands of miles, sniffing their way back to the mouth of their native stream with ease. Matching smells in the water with those they remember from their youth, the salmon start upstream, hurdling every obstacle in their path in their search for the exact tributary. All of this is done through an extraordinary sense of smell based on the imprints received during their early days of existence. Once back home, the salmon spawn to renew the eternal cycle of life. Pacific salmon quietly give up life once they've spawned. Atlantic salmon may return to the sea and eventually migrate back to the tributary to spawn a second or even a third time.

Red-backed sockeye salmon glut the river by the thousand on their long spawning journey back to the breeding grounds where they were born. The salmon find their way by smell alone. ▶

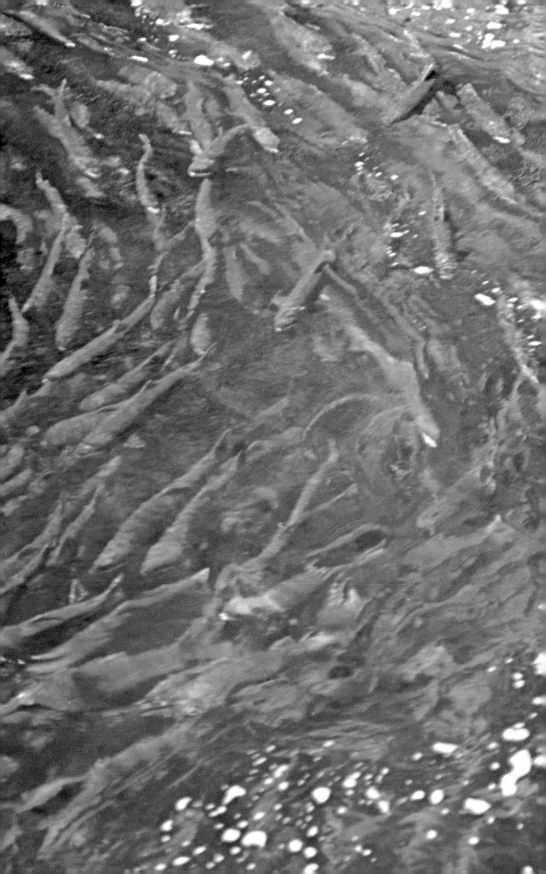

Prized gamefish of Canadian rivers, the hook-jawed Atlantic salmon relies on smell to find its spawning grounds; once there, the males are spurred to sexual activity by the odor of the females.

In recent years, commercial fishing for the Atlantic salmon has spread to the high seas and particularly in the Davis Straits off Greenland where stocks of fish intermingle to feed. This practice is extremely dangerous because the netting is indiscriminate and stocks of salmon from marginal spawning grounds can inadvertently be wiped out. Recent evidence also demonstrates that a significant number of fish are injured in the netting process and a great number of the fish taken are small, indicating that they may not have been back to the rivers to spawn. Where commercial fishing for salmon takes place in normal fashion at the river mouths, it can be regulated to permit enough of the spawners to get through.

Once salmon reach breeding grounds, their sense of smell, finds a new use in mating. The male Atlantic salmon, for example, is stimulated into a sexual mood by the odor of the females. Male shad also appear to react this way and certain gobies are also aroused sexually by the odor of the female. In other species, the reverse is true. An odor given off by the male will excite the female.

Modern research is constantly turning up new facts about the sense of smell in fish. Yet the subject isn't new by any means and even old-time anglers were well aware that they could catch more fish by appealing to their quarry's sense of smell. Way back in 1744, Munro said, " ... after the same Worm has been a considerable Time in the Water and lost its Smell, no Fishes will come near it, but if you take out the Bait and make several little Incisions into it so as to let out more of the odoriferous Effluvia, it shall have the same effect as formerly. . . "

No one really knows what it is in human saliva that will trigger a response from fish, but there's an old saying that if you want to catch catfish, spit on the bait. You don't have to tell the catfish angler that the best baits reek with odor. In fact, they are often referred to as "stink baits" because of the smell. But taste is involved too in the degree of attractiveness of odiferous baits to fish, and only with a scientist's approach can one begin to separate such closely related functions.

In an extensive and carefully controlled set of experiments, one scientist taste-tested sixty catfish with a list of natural substances. His goal was to determine which of the substances stimulated the appetites of the catfish the most. Worms and liver prove the most attractive, but the third item is the one that surprised everyone. Human saliva proved to be the third most attractive substance to catfish. So the next time you see someone spitting on a hunk of bait you'll know that there is sound technique behind his superstition.

5

Hearing

Of all the sensory systems of fish, hearing is the most versatile. Even when vision is obscured as the turbidity of water changes, the day becomes night, or the clean body of water flows into a muddy or polluted stretch, the hearing functions of fish adapt and remain acute. This auditory system is so precise that it enables a fish to hear sounds we cannot hear, and most of these sounds trigger a reaction.

One type of sound will signal the approach of a bait school. Another may arouse curiosity. Fear, brought about by other sounds, may send a fish to the safety of the nearest cover.

Because sounds do affect fish, that knowledge can be put to good use by fishermen.

Let's take the finicky brown trout as an example. It is essentially a night feeder, especially when it reaches heavy-weight proportions, and therefore relies heavily on its sense of smell. When it invades the shallows after baitfish, the brownie will use its senses of smell and hearing to home in on the target. The fly fisherman who chases brown trout after dark prefers large streamer or skimmer patterns that land with a "splat" and produce a husky silhouette as they skitter across the surface. The object is to appeal to the brown's senses of hearing and sight.

Basically, sounds transmitted into the water can either repel or attract fish. The trick, of course, is to avoid driving fish away with the wrong kind of sound and instead to arouse their curiosity or gain their attention with the right type of sound. We know that sound travels five times faster in the water than it does in the air, and we also are aware that fish are extremely sensitive to a wide range of frequencies. Interestingly enough, you'll seldom see a fish make a mistake and run toward an alarming sound. He immediately moves away from it. Yet, the gentle splat of a lure or bait at a respectable distance from the fish will often attract its attention, and there are some fish that will charge the offering without hesitation.

You may have observed this firsthand. If you haven't, toss a small pebble near a fish and watch what happens. Before the ripple clears, the fish is long gone. The same thing happens when you drop a lure too close to a fish. Its initial response is to flee. It doesn't matter how small the lure or how big the fish.

Largemouth bass fishermen sometimes drop lure or bait alongside a stump or other underwater obstruction where a bass is likely to be lying. To make matters worse, they often pop the lure loudly after it lands. Unfortunately, the angler seldom sees the results of his effort. A better approach is to cast a short distance from the bass lair and then cover that area during the retrieve.

Perhaps the most vivid examples of the effects of sound on fish occur on shallow saltwater flats or in a clear stream or lake, where an angler can easily observe exactly what happens. A school of 100-pound tarpon can be flushed by the sound of a lure landing too close, a lure weighing only a quarter of an ounce. In school behavior, if one fish becomes alarmed and spooks, the others will instantly react. It is vital when casting to a school of fish—particularly in shallow water—to avoid scaring any member of the school.

It is important to recognize from the outset that sound travels five times faster in water than it does in the air, at a rate of approximately one mile per second. Because water is an excellent conductor of sound waves but a very poor transmitter of light waves, fish have been endowed with an exceptionally good sense of hearing. Sensitivity will vary from species to species, but fish usually hear the best in the range of 200 to 800 cycles per second (middle C on the piano is 256 cycles per second). However, most fish can discern sounds over a much wider range, encompassing a minimum of 30 cycles per second to a maximum of about 2,000 cycles per second (about two octaves above middle C).

Some species have an auditory sense that can hear sounds down to about 15 cycles per second and higher than 10,000 cycles per second. If you are wondering how this compares to our own hearing, consider that the average person can hear from approximately 20 cycles to 20,000 cycles per second. Most commercial AM radio stations cannot reproduce sound over 10,000 cycles.

FISH HAVE EARS

Although fish don't have protruding earflaps like those of humans and other mammals, they do have ears and good ones. The hearing apparatus of a fish is a highly developed sense organ, so sensitive that it can sense the noise of a worm wiggling in the bottom.

The ears are buried on either side of the head in roughly the same position in which our own inner ears are found, but much closer together. Unlike us, fish do not have eardrums and the ears are not open to the water on the outside. Sounds are transmitted directly from the water through the skin, flesh, and bone of the fish's head to the ear.

Fish species that inhabit fast-moving water or a turbulent surf have little need for sensitive hearing. But those fishes that normally make their home in more quiet waters where low-key and subtle sounds are not masked by the roaring turbulence of water flow, waves, or tidal action, boast acute hearing ability.

Fish anatomists tell us that one clue to extremely sensitive hearing in certain species is an internal connection between the ear and the swim bladder. Because the swim bladder is a gas-filled chamber enclosed by an elastic membrane, it serves as an underwater microphone, resonating chamber, and amplifier all rolled into one. The bladder picks up vibrations from the water and transmits them directly to the ear. It has been proven that fish with this connection are very sensitive to soft sounds and can perceive intensities of 30 decibels lower than those species without it.

We find both predators and peaceful grazers in the group of species that benefits from swim-bladder-augmented hearing. High-sensitivity hearing is a valuable asset to the hunted as well as the hunter.

LATERAL LINE

In addition to their ears, fish have a second sound-detecting organ known as the lateral line which is unique in the animal kingdom. This organ senses the strong, low-frequency vibrations in the water and is important to a fish in pinpointing the source of a sound. The lateral line starts on the head as a network of tiny canals running just under the surface of the skin. Right behind the head, the canals join together forming the lateral line proper, which extends down each side of the fish to the tail. Perhaps the most vivid example occurs on the snook, a popular saltwater fish found in tropical waters, where the lateral organ is a strong black line on a lighter body and becomes the most obvious identifying mark of the species. The lateral line is present in some form on most every species and is easily discernible on trout or largemouth bass, showing as a delicate line running along the entire side of the fish.

Sound sensors, called neuromasts, are attached at intervals within the lateral line canals and are especially sensitive to low-frequency sounds. They are composed of tiny pods (cupolas) with sensory hairs inside. Each pod connects to a nerve fiber which carries signals to the brain. Sound vibrations in the water pass through thousands of openings along the lateral line and reach the sensory cells in the canal. There is a continuous pulsation of electric charges working along the nerves to feed the neuromasts. When the sound wave reaches the neuromasts, it will push them in one direction or the other. If the neuromasts are moved rearward, the electrical charges increase. If they move forward, the charges decrease.

Some scientists refer to the lateral line as "the sense of distant touch." It's almost as if a fish could reach out and feel.

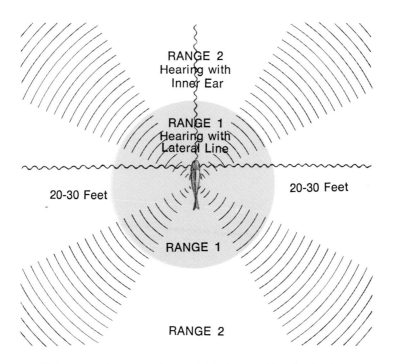

Fish can locate sounds in a restricted range (1) using the lateral line detector. At distances beyond 30 feet (Range 2), they detect sound with the inner ear, but cannot locate the source without swimming a search pattern.

Of particular significance to the angler is the distinction made between near-field sound and far-field sound. Near-field sound is created when the molecules of water are displaced by strong pressure waves. As the water is pushed along, it disturbs the neuromasts, which instantly detect the movement as low-frequency sound. These displacement waves which create near-field sound carry only a short distance through water. Depending on their force, they may reach out 20, 30, or perhaps 50 feet.

While the lateral line handles the near-field sounds, the ears concentrate on far-field sounds. Far-field sounds are created by pressure waves that force the water molecules to vibrate back and forth but without moving in any direction. These far-field pressure waves, sensed by the ears, are capable of traveling through the water for many miles and provide the fish with long-range hearing.

The lateral line thus supplements the ear by providing a super-sensitive system for detecting close disturbances in the water that create low-frequency sound waves—those that range from 200 down to 10 or 15 cycles per second. At the lowest of these frequencies, the laterial line senses sound that the ear cannot hear.

One peculiarity of the lateral line sensing system is its sensitivity for larger objects. This means that a larger predator or baitfish can be located at a greater distance and with greater accuracy than a smaller one. A preyfish can gain the advantage over a predator when both are using the lateral line for sensing in murky water or at night, because the smaller fish will hear the larger one first. Baitfish also have the advantage in moving water where the background noise is high, since the near-field vibrations of the predator are stronger and easier to detect than the weaker ones of the baitfish. However, it should be kept in mind that schools of fish produce a cumulative effect and a large school of small baitfish should produce a pronounced near-field sound.

HOW SOUND AFFECTS FISH

Sound plays a vital role in the daily activities of fish. Through the combined use of the ears and the lateral line, they can detect any disturbance in the water.

Fortunately, sound carried in the air, such as normal talking between fishermen—which registers about 25 decibels—does not affect fish at all. The water's surface will reflect 99.9 percent of the sound energy in the air. But man-made sounds are transmitted easily into the water through adjacent solid objects—rocks, the bank, or a boat floating on the surface.

Sounds transmitted through the water are equally significant to the freshwater angler pursuing panfish, bass, pike, or trout. Everyone has heard of the old Indian trick of putting an ear to the ground to detect footsteps a long way off. With water lying against the bank of the lake or stream, your footsteps are quickly carried by the water and picked up by the fish if you walk too close to the bank or shore. So, if you're going to approach a stream or lake, or you're changing locations, take the long way around. Walk a considerable distance from the bank and you won't have to worry about sound being transmitted to the fish.

Since the lateral line is directional, a fish can detect and sense the direction of a baitfish or lure quite well by using its lateral line at distances up to 10 or even 20 feet. Vibrations in the water caused by a lure or a fish would be of low frequency and the lateral line works best well below 200 cycles per second. At very close range—say 2 to 5 feet—a fish can precisely pinpoint another fish or a lure without using its eyes at all. Within 5 feet, a fish can whirl around and strike a lure or bait as easily as you can pick something up and put it in your mouth.

At distances greater than 20 to 30 feet, the lateral line has little value. Near-field sound is gone, and the lateral line has little value as a direction finder with sound above 200 cycles per second. It is believed that a fish lacks directional ability if it has to rely solely on its ears. In this range, the fish would depend on its ears to detect sound, but it could not locate the source.

Thus, at any distance beyond 20 or 30 feet, the fish could hear the sound and perhaps recognize its source, associating it with food, fear, sex, or something else, but it could not *locate* the source. If the object is close enough, the fish might be able to see it. If the sound were continuous, the fish could track it with its ears and determine if the sound were intensifying or lessening. That is, by moving in one direction or another, the fish could judge whether the sound was becoming louder or softer—and gradually locate the source.

MOTOR BOATS

Any boat is a resonator that will magnify and transmit sound into the water. That means that if you scrape a tacklebox along the bottom of the boat or shuffle your feet, the sound will reach the fish and could frighten them. You can do all the talking you want because it will bounce off the water's surface, but any movement in the boat is magnified by a sounding board effect.

Biologist James Moulton, studying the effect of sound on fish, discovered that fish exhibited obvious fright reactions when he merely flexed his knees as he stood in a 21-foot boat. In Moulton's words, "Just a shallow knee-bend with no foot movement spooked the fish." It's pretty tough to keep from moving while fishing, but Moulton's experiences point up the fact that an angler should try to eliminate as many noises as possible. One way of doing this is to pad the bottom of your tacklebox with soft material such as indoor-outdoor carpeting. You can do the same thing to boat decks. The effect is to muffle the sounds and this does help. In the excitement of casting from a small skiff, the angler often tries to put strength into the cast by shifting weight rapidly. This creates sound vibrations through the hull and we have seen several instances where the quarry was frightened before the lure hit the water.

In relatively still water, the effects of these sounds will be perceived by most fishes. Fish are particularly on the alert for strange, sharp sounds, especially those around 1,000 cycles that approximate the tail thump of an attacking predator.

The next time you are in shallow water where you can see some distance ahead, try standing in the bow of an outboard-powered skiff while someone runs it at about two-thirds throttle. Look into the water in front of the boat and if there are fish around, you'll see them streaking off in panic. This is equally true in either fresh or salt waters. There are times when an outboard won't seem to bother fish to any great degree; for example, over deeper water where they have plenty of room to maneuver and feel a degree of safety. Occasionally a constant traffic of outboards on the water conditions the fish and they ignore the noise. But in the majority of fishing situations, if you run an outboard over fish, they are going to flee. An outboard creates high-frequency sound and the fish will hear it with their ears a long distance off.

Knowing that, a fisherman who concentrates on the shallows will either use a pushpole or paddle. But if he happens to bang the pushpole against the side of the boat, the sound is instantly transmitted into the water and will scare the fish. Some anglers put crutch tips on the end of the forked shoe of a pushpole to deaden the sound of the pole against the bottom. Even a rowboat can be a frustrating craft, because the squeaking of the oarlocks is carried into the water through the hull.

Freshwater bass fishermen have been using electric motors in shallow water. The vibrations from electric motors are less offensive to fish, and the angler has an opportunity to approach his target without first alerting it. Although a fish may not immediately spook at the sound of a foreign noise, it often becomes alert and is much harder to fool into taking a bait or lure.

DISTRESS VIBRATIONS

Nothing can trigger a response in fish faster than the vibrations set up by an injured fish. The sounds produced by a wounded fish are totally different from those created when a fish is swimming normally.

Expert diver and fish observer Ray Hoglund proved that the vibrations of wounded baitfish do attract gamefish: "A walleye with one pectoral fin clipped short and his dorsal fin removed, taken into the water, flutters about trying to maintain his balance. The vibrations sent out as a result of his fluttering draw musky. The same principle holds true for bass. I tried drawing bass to me by breaking the back of a large roach minnow, putting it on a line, and taking it with me underwater. A bass rushed up, and although well-fed, struck the roach instantly. This I have done many times, with the same results. Beyond doubt, predatory fish are attracted by vibrations given off by another fish in distress."

One reason that fishing with live bait is so successful is that when you put a hook through the bait, you restrict its swimming ability and it sends out vibrations signalling that it is in trouble. A northern pike, walleye, trout, perch, largemouth, or any of the other freshwater fish senses these vibrations and moves toward their source. Not very long ago, we were fishing for big northern pike in Ontario's Bear Paw Lake. As we worked the shoreline casting Daredevils, Ray Peck, our host, hooked a small northern. While the northern flopped around on the surface of the water noisily, Ray tried to get a grip on it. As he reached down to release the fish, he let out a howl. Another pike of at least 20 pounds had engulfed two-thirds of the smaller fish and was trying to swallow it in one gulp. No doubt the vibrations of a fish in trouble helped the big predator to home in on what it considered an easy meal. But we were never able to get that heavyweight to hit one of our lures.

If you enjoy fishing live bait, you can often do much better by keeping the bait on the surface and working it so that it will flutter and splash. A gamefish will be attracted by the sound first, but because the bait is on the surface and silhouetted against the sky, the predator will switch quickly from sound sensing to vision and the attack should be swift.

If you don't have live bait and happen to be fishing from a bridge, you can sometimes accomplish the same effect with a whole dead bait. The trick is to let out just enough line to keep the bait on the surface just below where you are standing. Then, by manipulating the rod tip, you can make the bait jiggle and dance. You can't set up the same vibrations as a wounded or hooked fish, but you can often create enough commotion to attract a hit. Some bridge anglers practice a technique often referred to as "bridge trolling" in which they walk back and forth across the bridge keeping the dead bait "swimming" on the surface.

An example of distress vibrations occurred with regularity while we were fishing live bonito for black marlin off the Pacific coast of Panama. The big blacks frequent a rise in the sea floor known as Pinas Reef. The reef is alive with all species of fish, and the surface is frequently covered with acres of bonito. There's enough natural bait to fill the bellies of all the black marlin in the area. Yet, the technique is to catch a live bonito, sew it on a hook, and then troll it slowly along the edge of the huge school of bonito.

Invariably, when the fishing is hot, your bait isn't in the water long before a black marlin is zeroing in on it. Anglers who don't understand that an injured fish sends out special vibrations are puzzled that a black marlin finds that one bonito out of a school of thousands. Any gamefish is looking for an easy meal, and the marlin instinctively knows that it takes much less effort to run down a prey that is handicapped.

The technique of kite fishing in salt water uses sound to attract the big gamesters. The sound of a baitfish fluttering on the surface proves irresistible to many species and prompts them to come topside for a look. In kite fishing, live baits are worked on the surface where they can flutter and send out those magical vibrations. The kite is flown from a boat, and there are a pair of clothespins attached to the kite string (actually heavier line). By adjusting the length of line from the rod and reel through the clothespin and to the bait, the angler can keep the bait on the surface of the water.

SOUNDS MADE BY FISH

Fish not only hear sounds, they make sounds. Biologists classify these sounds as either mechanical or biological in origin. Mechanical sounds are made accidentally by fish that are chewing, spawning, chasing prey, or foraging on the bottom. When a fish tries to communicate with its schoolmates or another fish, the sound is considered biological. Biological sounds, then, are fish voices. These vocalizations are accomplished by a number of different methods. One way is by muscular drumming of the swim bladder. Another is by gnashing the pharyngeal teeth (throat or gill teeth), and a third is by rubbing certain bones of the body together.

Fish, like birds and land animals, make biological sounds for a variety of reasons. Many species have a mating call which they use to attract their mates at spawning time. Some use sound signals to locate each other and keep their schools intact. Others resort to sound as a means of territorial defense to warn an intruder. There are even a few species that seem to use echo-ranging systems to locate objects underwater by sending out signals which bounce off other fish, the bottom, or obstructions that are out of the range of vision. Thus, some fish, just like bats and the familiar air-breathing dolphin, can swim about keeping track of the world by sonar.

Biologists who have recorded fish voices with hydrophones describe these biological sounds as grunts, growls, squeaks, clicks, knocks, boops, raps, rasps, scratches, honks, whistles, hums, hisses, purrs, and so on. But only a few of the popular game species number among the more notable sound producers. Jacks make a rasping or a rattling sound with the pharyngeal teeth. Bonefish make loud growls and thumps. Striped bass can make single, low-frequency thumps at 75 to 300 cycles per second by contracting their body muscles and squeezing the air bladder when they are annoyed or startled. Catfish, minnows, haddock, and grunts also contribute sounds to the chorus. Few people realize that it takes tremendous power to produce sound underwater. It is 150,000 times more difficult to produce sound in water as it is in air.

Most underwater sound is only audible below the surface, but a dramatic exception is the "drumming" of the black drum. Anglers fishing for this saltwater species often hear fish that are down in relatively deep water. The sound is similar to that produced by a youngster blowing air into a soda bottle—a deep, hollow sound—and it echos through the hull of the boat. When you hear the sound of the drum, you often catch fish.

The popular seatrout (spotted weakfish) is a well-known sound maker. Professor Charles Fish reports the following observations:

> During July, when gonads were ripening, males croaked freely with little stimulation. When pursued, these specimens produced bursts of loud croaking, and after capture, they re-

peated the sounds with every movement of the containing net. Transfer to another aquarium was accompanied by continuous clucking. An accidental collision with a tankmate was sufficient to evoke a single loud croak. Sometimes, this was followed by a burst of clucking. The female, however, produced sound only on one occasion, when a striped bass jostled her out of hiding in a corner. A single low cluck coincided with her quick turn to escape, after which a short series of sounds followed in a higher pitch.

In Ghana, on the Atlantic coast of Africa, fishermen listen for fish with an odd-looking paddle shaped like a large version of a three-tined wooden picnic fork. This instrument is so sensitive to underwater vibrations that fishermen can not only hear fish, but can locate them with it. The paddle blade acts as a sounding board which receives sound signals and transmits them up the handle. An experienced man can put the paddle in the water at the stern of his canoe, press his ear to the handle, and by rotating the paddle determine the direction of a school of fish. They have even refined the basic technique. The intensity of the sound received indicates the size of the school and the distance from the canoe. Oddly enough, the system works best in about 60 feet of water and during the earliest hours of the morning.

There are two types of mechanical sounds made by fishes as they swim. The first category includes vibrations of various frequencies and intensities resulting from a disturbance in the water as the fish pass through it or maneuver about. A second category includes the less audible sounds made by the muscles and joints as a fish swims. Mechanical sounds are audible to many other fish. Biologist James Moulton was able to record the swimming sounds of anchovy, jacks, and pompano around Bermuda and off New York's Long Island by using a hydrophone and a tape recorder. The anchovy, a baitfish, made no noise while at rest, but according to Moulton, they made "considerable sound" while swimming ahead and changing direction. The most intense sound occurred below a frequency of 500 cycles per second, well inside the range of sharp hearing of most predatory gamefish.

In another experiment, Moulton played the taped sounds of anchovies swimming to a school of young jacks. The jacks immediately became excited and swam rapidly around the tank in a search pattern, or, as Moulton put it: "They showed quickening movements of a non-directional type." These and similar experiments demonstrate that even when crude recordings of swimming noises are played back to gamefish, they hear and respond. One of these days, an enterprising angler may even resort to a tape recorder and sound to improve his catch.

The most pronounced mechanical sounds recorded from the jacks and pompanos were loud thumps made with their tails during sharp turns (known scientifically as veering). The jacks also made biological stridulation sounds by scraping their pharyngeal teeth together. When Moulton played back these stridulations, either alone or in combination with the tail thumps, the baitfish became alarmed and fled from the underwater speaker. Apparently, they recognized and were disturbed by the noise of the predatory jacks.

While in Bermuda, Moulton attracted a hungry barracuda by playing tape recordings of jack noises. The large predator came quickly and headed directly for the underwater speaker. It remained in position 8 feet away from the puzzling artificial sound maker for several minutes until it decided that it wasn't a meal. The incident was also observed by the boat's experienced skipper, Brunell Spurling, who commented that he had never in his life seen any barracuda behave in that manner.

Underwater fish watcher Ray Hoglund has lain quietly on the bottom with the aid of scuba gear and tapped two stones together, attracting swarms of bass, crappies, perch, rock bass and bluegills. Yet the instant he moved or changed positions, the fish would scatter in all directions. Working in conjunction with another diver who remained in the boat and followed the progress on an extremely sensitive recording fathometer, Hoglund found that when he was swimming in open water, his own vibrations alarmed fish. The fish would continuously swim a considerable distance in front of him, off in the gloom beyond the range of his visibility. While snorkeling underwater, we have heard the powerful thumps from striped bass that we never saw, thumps that carried like sonic booms as their powerful tails lashed the water.

Fish are sensitive to all sounds that have meaning to them. Carp are attracted by playbacks of the sounds of other carp eating or even of other carp swimming. Trout, too, react positively to tapes of the sounds of other trout eating and swimming. Yellowtail jacks, attracted to playbacks of recorded eating and swimming sounds of other jacks, have become so excited in some experiments that they even tried to bite the sound speakers. Mackerel can be frightened into panic and driven into nets by playbacks of the sounds made by porpoises, a feared predator.

SIMULTANEOUS FEEDING

The mysterious way in which all the fish in a lake begin to feed at one time may very well be due to hearing. Fish are competitive about feeding. They have to be to survive. A fish can easily be provoked into feeding when he sees or *hears* another fish start feeding. It is extremely possible that a few fish can start a chain reaction. When fish are actively feeding, the sound of their tail thumps or surface splashings travel through the water at the rate of one mile per second. On a calm evening, all the fish in a small lake could hear and react to one sharp tail thump within a few seconds. You know how easily you can hear the sound of breaking fish on a calm day. Imagine what it must sound like underwater!

Although research in the vast field of sound has not been as thorough as the need dictates, there is little doubt that sound with all its ramifications is a critical factor in the life of a fish and it is equally critical from a fisherman's standpoint. As a fisherman, you should be aware of the effects of sound and make them work for you both in attracting fish and by avoiding those sounds that would have an adverse effect and frighten fish.

6

Taste, Touch and Temperature Perception

Most fishermen recognize that the "S-Group" of senses—sight, smell, and sound perception—play a major role in the feeding and defensive patterns of most fish. In fact, we have already demonstrated that a fish's final attack on a bait or lure is often based on sight, although its interest was perhaps originally aroused by sound or smell. There are many species, however, that can actually find food by touch. Still others taste their food with external detectors *before* actually putting it in their mouths.

This secondary group of senses is of paramount importance to numerous species, yet the majority of anglers are either unaware of its existence or fail to consider it seriously. Scientifically, the "T-Group" senses—taste, touch, and temperature perception—are known as the cutaneous senses.

TASTE AND SMELL

Like the sense of smell, taste is classified as a "chemo-receptor" because it detects the presence of chemical substances in the water. Both smell and taste are closely related in fish just as they are among humans. We could describe smell as a long-range or distant receptor, while taste is the close-up, or contact receptor. Said another way, fish use smell in the process of searching out their food and then employ taste to determine if it is acceptable.

A gamefish that attacks a live bait or strikes a lure isn't worried about taste during the attack. The fish knows instinctively that most live or moving creatures in the water are a source of food and the first impulse is to strike the object. Suppose that the moving object is a painted hunk of wood or plastic with two or three sets of treble hooks hanging from its body. Or possibly it's a dry fly carefully fashioned from hair and feathers. When the fish ingests this offering, he realizes almost immediately that it's not the real thing and he generally tries to eject it just as quickly. Fishermen speak of this common occurrence in terms of "feel." The lure doesn't feel natural to the fish. But in many cases, the lure may simply not *taste* like anything that would be appetizing.

This, of course, is theory, but we mention it because we do know that fish can discriminate between different taste sensations. To demonstrate this, a group of scientists experimented with minnows from which they had removed the odor section of the brain. This meant that the fish had no power of smell. Yet the minnows were able to discriminate between sweet, sour, salty, and bitter tastes.

It's important to realize that even in humans, taste is a nebulous sense. The four basic distinctions of sweet, sour, salty, and bitter can be made, but a food that tastes appetizing to one person, may be repulsive to another.

The relation of smell to taste among fish is an important consideration when fishing natural bait. Live bait, of course, won't present problems in this quarter. But, if you are using dead bait, it should always be the freshest available. Frequently, an angler will begin the day with fresh bait, but because he uses poor methods for keeping it fresh, he could be missing out on catching fish. Sun, heat, and even fresh water from melted ice, in the case of saltwater baits, can make a difference. Dead bait should be preserved as well as possible until its moment of use. And although thawed frozen bait is better than stale bait, it still isn't as good as fresh bait that hasn't been frozen.

EXTERNAL TASTE BUDS

The organs of taste in fishes are taste buds similar to our own. However, the taste buds of fish are not limited to the tongue and palate as they are in humans. Just where they occur on any type of fish depends on its particular way of life and method of feeding. The majority of fish have external taste buds on the lips and snout as well as internal ones in the mouth and throat. Some have taste buds on chin feelers, fins, or other parts of the body. These microscopic taste buds are shaped like tiny closed tulip buds. Each connects to a nerve axis that delivers taste sensations to the rear of the brain—a part called the medulla.

Through the external taste buds, fish can test and taste their food by simply touching it with their snouts or another part of their body that has similar taste buds. So the taste sensation really starts when a fish gets close to its food, intensifies as contact is made, and continues even more strongly as it ingests its food.

To a fisherman, the fact that a fish can taste a bait without ever taking it in its mouth can present problems and frustrations. If a fish had to mouth a bait to taste it, you would have time to set the hook. But when he merely has to nose the bait to sample the flavor, there is nothing to be done if he rejects it. If you see a fish nose the bait and swim away, you know that something is wrong with the offering—either it appears unnatural or it is not as fresh as it should be.

Catfish has the most sensitive taste equipment in the fish world, with most of its taste buds concentrated in the barbels, or feelers, that hang from its jaw.

Catfish are the taste champions of the world of fish. A single catfish has as many as 100,000 taste buds scattered over its body. Most of them are concentrated in the barbels, or feelers, that protrude on either side of the jaw like the whiskers on a cat. There are usually eight of these barbels that serve as external tongues, tasting various items in the water. With these barbels, catfish continuously test the water and the bottom mud to detect any taste of food. Without taste-sensitive barbels, species that live and feed on soft mud bottoms would have a serious handicap. As the fish roots around for its food, it stirs up clouds of silt. The silt not only interferes with vision, making it impossible to see food, it also fills the water with a variety of organic smells that ooze from the bottom mud when it is disturbed. Odor perception becomes instantly confused. With vision and smell rendered useless much of the time, it is quite an advantage for the catfish to be able to taste its way around.

Catfish rely so heavily on their barbels for feeding that without them they could not locate any food. This was emphatically demonstrated in a series of experiments. Scientists removed the barbels of a group of test fish, and when the fish were offered live worms, they were unable to locate them. A second group of test fish was introduced in which their barbels were intact but the smell center in their brain had been disconnected. These fish had no trouble locating the worms and ingesting them, proving that taste and not smell was the key sense in their feeding.

Since catfish normally taste or feel their food with their barbels, it stands to reason that they are more apt to locate bait that is on or near the bottom. They feed primarily on the bottom, and if the bait is suspended too far above their normal feeding zone, they may miss it.

In addition to catfish, many other species that feed in dim light or in muddy water also have taste buds on special appendages. The carp is a familiar example in fresh water. This species roots around in the mud for its food; best baits are doughballs of cornmeal and flour. Also consider the sturgeon and, in salt water, the mullet, sea robin, goatfish, cod, and black drum. Some of these species have taste buds concentrated on chin barbels like the catfish, while others have them on fingerlike extensions of their pelvic fins with which they walk over the bottom, tasting as they go.

It is natural for us as humans to think of the fish's response to food as a sudden whiff, a fast grab, and a quick taste as it goes down. In reality, the process is much more methodical, particularly with the species that are primarily smell-taste feeders.

The chain of response starts when the fish smells something that interests it. Becoming alert to the presence of food, it swims faster and begins to track down the source like a bird dog on the scent. Once its target is located, the fish first tests the nature of the substance with the external taste buds on its snout, barbels, or fins. If the fish likes what it finds, it puts the bait to the final test by deftly taking it into its mouth. At this moment, it will finally decide either to swallow the bait or spit it out.

SENSE OF TOUCH

Touch is the T-Group sense often referred to as the tactile sense. In scientific circles it is generally known that most fish do not have the sensitivity of touch that we know as humans. But because there has been a lack of experimentation in this area, no one really knows how effectively fish use this sense for feeding or defending themselves. Bottom species seem to find touch useful for navigating and moving along the bottom among rocks and other obstacles.

The courtship of many fishes involves a good deal of rubbing, brushing, and general body contact wherein touch is obviously important. Other behavior patterns such as the schooling and nesting of certain species also involve touch.

Half a mackerel on a teasing rig brushes the fins of a hammerhead shark and sends it on a feeding spree. Sharks have sensitive organs of touch over their entire body, especially on their fins.

And you know that when you touch a fish, it is generally responsive and will react. Yet, in most species of fish, there is little evidence of highly developed touch receptors in the skin.

Of primary concern to fishermen, however, is the use of touch as it relates to feeding. As you would expect, bottom species and those fish that specialize in feeding in dim light seem to have a more functional sense of touch. Freshwater catfish are reported to have sensitive tactile organs on their heads, lips, and barbels which they use along with the highly developed chemical sensors (smell and taste) to locate and test potential items for food. The moray eels are notorious night feeders that appear to have sensitive snouts for actually touching and feeling their food. Sharks also are reported to have sensitive organs of touch, especially on their fins, which probably come into play during feeding.

TEMPERATURE PERCEPTION

The final sense in the T-Group, temperature perception, operates with surprising precision. Using the "conditioned reflex" method of experiments, behavioral scientists have found that both fresh- and saltwater species can easily sense a change in temperature as minute as a fraction of 1 degree Fahrenheit.

Fish detect temperature through impulses sent to the brain by a network of tiny nerve endings in the skin surface. These nerves not only detect temperature changes, but discriminate between a temperature rise or fall. Although scientists are aware of the ability of most fish species to do this, they still do not understand the physiological or biochemical process involved in the operation of the temperature sensing system.

Temperature sensitivity was first tested by a British researcher, H. O. Bull, who trained cod to leave their tank and wiggle up a ramp to get a bite of food whenever he changed the temperature slightly. By constantly working to perfect their response, Dr. Bull was able to get them to react when he changed the temperature as little as 1/50 of a degree Farenheit. This incredible sensitivity is not matched by man or any warm-blooded creature that we know.

Elsewhere in this book, we have described the effects of temperature on fish as it pertains to their habitat. Although fish like the cod can perceive minute changes in temperature, they do not necessarily react to these changes every time or even most times. In their normal lives, most fish must go about their business quite oblivious to changes of less than ½ degree. But in some species, the ability to detect these slight temperature changes is significant. They may be trying to navigate, for example, along a temperature gradient during an annual migration which requires precise temperature detection.

Being cold blooded, the body temperatures of fish are governed by the temperature of the surrounding water. This is a heat transfer process in which the water temperature either raises or cools the body temperature of the fish, speeding up or slowing down metabolic processes. The transfer of heat occurs through skin capillaries and through the large capillary bed of the gills. Remember, however, that the temperature adjustment is not an instant process and rapid temperature changes may produce fish kills because the fish simply cannot adjust to the change rapidly enough. Young fish with larger heads and gills in relation to their bodies can adjust to temperature changes better than adult fish with proportionately smaller gill areas. Passive temperature adjustment is based on body area and gill size.

This should not be confused with temperature changes within the fishes body caused by muscular activity or fright. It has been established, for example, that some species such as perch, sunfish, and even catfish will experience a slight rise in body temperature when they are alarmed.

Muscular activity also produces heat, and species such as the tunas and marlins have been known to raise their body temperatures from 12 to 15 degrees Fahrenheit during a hard-fought battle with an angler. This type of heat is a function of mass and occurs because the body of the fish cannot dissipate the heat created by muscular activity fast enough.

There are many scientists who believe that fish fight harder when the water is cooler, and that applies to warm-water and tropical fish as well. Of course, you must recognize that by cooler water we mean the lower end of the temperature preference range of a species and not arctic waters. Marlin, for example, taken on the edge of the cold Humboldt Current on the Pacific side of South America, will usually give a better account of themselves than the same species of fish taken in the warmer waters of Baja California.

Enough is already on record to prove that the cutaneous senses—taste, touch, and temperature perception are important considerations in any type of sport fishing.

7

Coloration and Camouflage

In the underwater world of fish there is little margin for error. Every fish must cope with enemies lurking below and above the surface, and every fish must feed successfully if it is to survive. Coloration and camouflage play a dual role in the survival strategy of most fish, protecting them from their enemies and giving them an advantage in ambushing their food.

A fish uses coloration for resemblance, for concealment, or as a signal. With a resemblance system, the fish attempts to appear as something else; for example, a pike lying motionless and appearing as a log in the water. There are saltwater species that look just like rocks on the bottom. Concealment, used for protection or for ambushing prey, is usually accomplished with camouflage patterns of body color that tend to make a fish inconspicuous. Repulsive, poisonous, or aggres-

sive fish often warn of their unpleasantness with flashy deco-
rations such as those of the fatally poisonous lionfish.

For the most part, though, our popular game species are
rather plain in coloration. In fact, the gamefishes, and particularly the saltwater species, usually lead simple lives,
depending upon speed and stamina, rather than cunning, for
their sustenance and defense. But still, each species has
evolved a protective pattern of some sort. Gamefish exhibit
bright colors to a limited degree, but seldom of the complex-
ity and specialization of non-game species such as tropical
reef dwellers.

The art of camouflage lies in confusing the vision of the
enemy so that it cannot see or recognize the prey for what it
really is. There are many different methods of visual decep-
tion, but all involve shape, color, and brightness.

COUNTERSHADING

The most common camouflage pattern for concealment is
countershading, a gradual shading of the fish from dark on
the upper surface to light underneath and across the belly.
Look down on a body of water from above and it appears to
be dark no matter how clear it really is. From the depths,
however, the water appears bright against the sky. That's the
reason for countershading and why practically every species
of fish is dark on top and light on the bottom.

A secondary effect of countershading is to remove any
appearance of dimension, causing the fish to look flat rather
than solid. Countershading compensates for light coming
from all directions. Called Thayer's Principle in honor of its
discoverer, this effect blends the light values along the flanks
of a fish to present an overall neutral tone with no distinct
break between upper and lower surfaces. In this way, the fish
can be nearly invisible from any angle of view. Logically, the
need for contrast diminishes with depth, and deeper-water
fish tend to forego the more complex systems of countershading.

Countershading is so successful a system that practically
every species has it to some degree. Any angler would be

The most common fish camouflage is countershading, a gradual lightening of color tone from dark above to pale below.

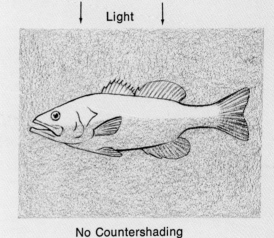

If a fish were not countershaded, it would be visible in the water because of sunlight from above.

No Countershading

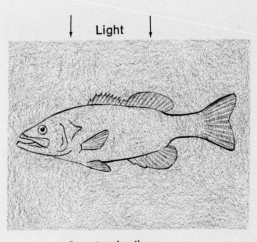

A countershaded fish appears neutral in tone and blends with the background. It is also camouflaged from above and below.

Countershading

Countershading shows clearly on these fish in a kelp forest owing to front lighting from the photographer's strobe. Normally, sunlight from above would neutralize graduated tone and fish would be less visible.

hard pressed to name a fish he has caught that did not at least have a lighter belly and darker top. Trout and salmon are clearcut examples of this form of coloration and are nearly impossible to see from above. In salt water, all of the pelagic game species employ distinctive countershading because they live above the bottom and have only the sky for cover when seen by a predator attacking from below. The striped bass has been nominated as a perfect example of a sophisticated system of countershading and camouflage.

Most freshwater anglers have a great deal of difficulty seeing fish in a stream, and a major reason is countershading. Brian Curtis, a trained biologist and expert fisherman, provides an example from his studies of trout spawning in a high

Sierra stream in California. When two barriers were erected
in the stream about thirty feet apart, Curtis thought he
noticed three trout accidentally slip in between the barriers
and enter an area where they weren't supposed to be. He
managed to catch two of them and release them again outside the barriers. Although Curtis caught glimpses of the
third fish during the next few weeks, he was unable to catch
it. The only alternative was to trap the fish. When Curtis
hauled the trap up next morning, he not only had the third
trout but five more—all about ten inches. He had not seen the
other five during a full month of patrolling a 30-foot stretch
of a tiny stream 8 feet wide and 2 feet deep.

DISRUPTIVE COLORATION

Many species use color patterning for concealment. This type
of camouflage is often called disruptive coloration because
the pattern disrupts an observer's view of the fish. It is typical
of fish that live around weed beds (pickerel), stumps and
rocks (bass), or reefs (groupers). In all of these places, the
background is laced with broken forms, irregular shadings,
and shifting shadows. Because almost any camouflage system
that breaks up the regularity of the body image will work,
one may see a limitless variety of patterns of color—bars,
stripes, patches, rings, spots, and swirls. Surface fish tend
toward cooler colors, blues and greens, while bottom dwellers sport the warmer colors, reds and browns.

The markings themselves are difficult to catalog, but we
have attempted to classify the more common ones.

> BARS: Roughly parallel vertical markings, dark on light or
> vice-versa.
> BANDS: Bars that completely encircle the body.
> STRIPES: Roughly parallel horizontal markings.
> SPOTS: Smallish round or oval markings, not arranged in rows
> (stripes) or columns (bars).
> PATCHES: Irregularly shaped and variable color markings.
> RINGS: Color rings, either circular or geometric.
> MARGINS: Fringing color at the edges of fins or other body
> parts.

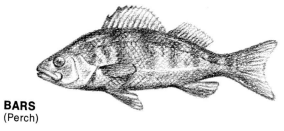

BARS
(Perch)

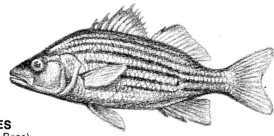

STRIPES
(Yellow Bass)

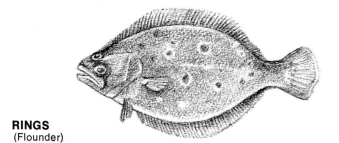

RINGS
(Flounder)

BANDS
(Grass Pickerel)

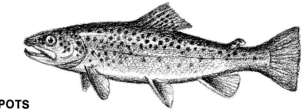

SPOTS
(Brown Trout)

◀ The more common types of disruptive coloration. Each breaks up the
fish's body in some way so it blends with the background.

   Sometimes the patterns appear to be random irregularities
but frequently they are so specific that you can relate fish to
their typical habitat on the basis of the markings alone. Consider the muskellunge. It has a pattern of thin, irregular, vertical bars covering most of its flanks. These side markings are
suggestive of the shadow pattern made by weed strands on
the lake bottom. The upper (dorsal) surface of a musky is
rather plain and dark so that its color resembles that of the
muddy bottom when viewed from above. Just by looking at a
muskie, you would conclude that it prefers a habitat of weed
beds because its sides are decorated to approximate the light
filtering through a weed bed and its back is dark like the
bottom.
   As you learn more about the muskie's strategy, you find
that the color pattern is for ambush purposes, not for protection—offense rather than defense. The muskie depends almost
wholly on ambush for capture of prey and spends long hours
lying in wait for a victim to swim within striking range. The
habit of the muskellunge to inspect its prey so thoroughly is
one reason they are so hard to catch on artificial lures in
comparison with the northern pike.
   In contrast to the patient muskie, the northern pike stalks
its prey in open waters, hovering over a gravel bed or near
the fringe of a weedy patch. In consequence, the northern is
patterned with spots, a camouflage system that is generalized
rather than specialized like the bars of the muskie, which are
designed for lurking in shadowy weed beds. The pike strikes
straight and fast like the muskie but attacks in the open and
runs down its prey after a chase. The pike's versatile color
pattern provides it with a degree of concealment wherever
it may be.
   There is obviously a great deal of randomness in the evolutionary sequence that led each species to the specific color

Perfectly colored to blend with the ocean floor, a flounder is barely visible to the camera's eye—or to the eyes of predators or prey.

Hovering near a weedbed, a northern pike waits patiently for a prey fish to swim by. The pike's spotted sides provide generalized camouflage for stalking and attacking prey in open waters.

Yellow grouper's blotchy coloration is admirably suited to the broken forms and shifting shadows of rocks and coral in its habitat. Lying quietly near the bottom, the grouper blends with its background.

pattern we see today. Evolution is an experiment in trial and error. Changes occur by genetic accident and remain locked in only if they are good for the species and improve its chances of survival. Otherwise, those of a species born with certain differences will not survive, and the differences will die out. When it comes to the point where any further development in a color pattern has no particular value to the survival of the species (and this takes eons of time), the pattern becomes permanent. In this way, each species evolves its definite pattern through a series of random accidents.

In apparent defiance of this rule, a whole new pattern can be created suddenly by an evolutionary short circuit caused by the crossbreeding of two separate species. But the crosses, or hybrids, are sterile and since they cannot breed more of their kind, nothing permanent comes of this biological accident.

Returning to our example of the "ripple-barred" muskie and the "spotted" pike, crossbreeding sometimes does take place in the grass beds where both species spawn. The result is the spectacular tiger muskellunge. The tiger has a pattern of bold stripes rather than the spots of one parent and the rippled bars of the other. There are some in the scientific community who claim the tiger is a proper subspecies rather than a sterile hybrid being continuously reproduced by crossbreeding of pike and muskellunge. Whether permanent or temporary, the half-breed tiger with its unique color pattern appears to be a success in its own right wherever it occurs.

Some biologists believe that the color pigments used by fish in their camouflage patterns originated for purposes other than protection. They claim that protective coloration is a side benefit and the substances that give color to a fish's body are there for other reasons. As an example, many are chemical pigments used for various physiological activities. Some have a specific purpose in relation to light, such as the reflection of excess light rays that could damage tissues or the absorption of light waves that might provide warmth. Regardless of the basic purpose of the pigments, nature has concentrated them and arranged them in unique patterns to provide the additional value of protective coloration.

VIVID COLORATION

In an apparent switch from the plain appearance of most surface-dwelling fishes, some saltwater species have evolved striking patterns of color on their upper sides. Ripples on the surface of the water break up the sun's rays and transform them into patterns of shimmering light and shadow. For deceptive camouflage, these patterns are matched by the various rippled bars, spots, or stripes on such species as the Spanish mackerel, little tuna, bonito, and wahoo. The prize for the most perfect ripple design, however, would have to go to the Atlantic (or Boston) mackerel.

Mackerel perform the dual role of super predator and super prey. They feed greedily on all the small life in the sea and they, in turn, are fed on voraciously by tunas, bluefish, striped bass, whales, and even gulls and fish hawks. To stay alive, they need maximum protection from above, below, and both sides. Their fancy coloration provides them with the high degree of camouflage they require—rippled on top, sky-colored underneath.

The most bizarre and striking color patterns are found on tropical reef fishes. Most reef fish feed by browsing on plant life, gulping fry, or attacking small shellfish, so they don't really need camouflage for ambush purposes. The reef is a patchwork of caves and niches. During the daylight hours, small fish find protection in these places and don't need the benefit of coloration for concealment. The water is so clear that these fish can see predators coming far enough away to run for cover.

However, the bright colors do have a purpose: they are primarily for identification. It is important for reef fish to be able to identify each other because they are territorial by nature and jealously guard their home grounds against invasion. Territorial threats usually come from their own species, and they will drive the invader off with vigor and swiftness of purpose. They will also attack similarly colored fish of another species. Yet, oddly enough, they usually won't bother fish with different color patterns that happen to stray into their territory.

Brightly colored tropical reef fish which browse on plant life and small fry have no need of camouflage coloration. Territorial by nature, reef fish identify each other by their vivid colors. They defend their home grounds against invaders of the same species, ignore members of other species.

Many reef fishes can alter their appearance dramatically by a rapid change of color pattern. One such master of the quick change is the Nassau grouper, a favorite of reef fishermen, which can choose between eight different mottled patterns, looking like a different species with each one. The Nassau grouper shifts patterns depending on whether it is feeding, hiding, wandering, or spawning, but its recognition mark—a dark spot on the back just ahead of the tail—always remains visible.

118

REFLECTIVE COLORATION

Up to this point, no mention has been made of the fishes that are silver colored beneath a dark upper surface. The dark top of the fish is certainly understandable as protection from predators above. But the silver sides would seem to be a poor defense. Actually, the silver pigment cells (called iridocytes) reflect the surrounding colors of the water and the bottom. The enemy does not really see an outline of its prey, but instead a reflection of the water. It's almost like hiding behind a mirror.

Anadromous salmon, trout, and Arctic char that are fresh from the sea are silver-sided, protective coloration against the larger predators that inhabit big water. Only after they enter the rivers and streams to spawn do the pigments change and spawning colors become pronounced.

From certain studies we know that underwater the body of a perch is so perfect a reflector, that except where the bars are present, it takes the exact shade of the water around. It is almost impossible to detect the fish's outline, and when looking at it from under the surface, through any extent of water, you see merely a few dark shadows moving along, such as might be caused by reeds or weeds.

Gliding across the Florida flats, the silver-sided tarpon is a prime example of a species that depends on reflective coloration for concealment. The silver sides of the fish reflect the surrounding water and vegetation, breaking up the outline of the body so an enemy sees only the reflection.

If you've stalked the glamorous bonefish or the tackle-busting tarpon on the shallow flats, no one need tell you how effective a silver body can be when it comes to camouflage. Even with polarized sunglasses, it takes practice to spot your quarry. Beginners do better over white sand bottoms. If the angle of observation is correct in relation to the sun, the fish will appear as dusky shapes ghosting along. But the instant the fish glide over a bottom of turtle grass or a mottled bottom of any type, you have to be very observant to keep them in view. The reflection from the bottom on the silver simply makes the fish vanish. Even the best flats fishermen will readily admit that schools of either bonefish or tarpon have moved within a few feet of the boat before they were seen.

WARNING COLORATION

So far, most of the discussion has centered on coloration and camouflage as a means of concealment either for protection or to make feeding easier. But concealment is only one benefit of color patterning. Another is advertisement (either as a warning or for signaling); the strategy, to be seen and recognized. In many respects, this is a distinct advantage. Earlier, we mentioned how repulsive or poisonous fishes warn off attackers or territorial invaders who automatically associate the bright patterns with trouble. But fish must be able to recognize their own kind for such mundane purposes as schooling and breeding. What better way to do this than to show a recognizable color pattern?

Some species combine the best of both worlds— concealment and signaling. For these fishes, most of the body is covered with concealment coloration, but there is a brightly colored signal marking somewhere on the body. The cleverest arrangement is to have signal markings on the fins, which can be retracted to hide the mark when there is danger.

A brook trout fisherman who has waded streams during the fall spawning season knows that the male becomes festooned in gaudy belly colors while the female is less pretentious. Males and females of many other species are often decorated

Well camouflaged for concealment in its weedy habitat, the bluegill also has a signal marking behind its gill, called an ear flap. The dark spot, which is a different size and shape on every species of sunfish, helps members of the same species to identify each other for purposes of schooling or breeding.

with different color patterns, proving that at times the need to recognize a mate is more important than the need for concealment coloration.

We have watched the rock-dwelling Atlantic blackfish (tautog) go through its spawning color stages in the sea tanks of the Narragansett Marine Gamefish Laboratory in Rhode Island. The males are always dark in color. Females are dark, too, with obscure bars during most of the year. But in the spring as the eggs develop and the urge to spawn comes on them, the females change color to signal their condition. Coloration becomes a contrasting pattern of dark bars on a light surface. Then, when they are ready to engage the males, they display a large white patch on a dark background. The males read the signal, surround the female, and in perfect formation the group rockets upward, spewing milt and eggs in a single crashing rush.

MOMENTARY COLOR CHANGES

In addition to their permanent color pattern, most species exhibit momentary intensities of color that can be highly significant to the fisherman skilled in recognizing these signs. For example, excitement causes the sides of billfish to brighten "as if a neon sign had been turned on." Experienced billfish anglers are well aware of this color change and refer to a fish as "lighting up."

While fishing for striped marlin off the coast of Salinas, Ecuador, the marlin we spotted at the surface were dark on the back and silvery on the sides, shading towards purple on the upper flanks. When the boat was guided past the fish and the baits swung over the transom, the marlin's sides turned a brilliant silver with gold bands. As the color flared, you could sense the excitement in the fish. A strike was seldom more than seconds away. But if the fish failed to light up, or faded after its initial invasion among the skipbaits, it meant that we hadn't convinced it that our offering was edible.

In the last few years, saltwater flyrodders have devised a method of taking amberjack on flyrod poppers with amazing regularity. It takes two fishermen for a successful venture, one to tease the fish while the other casts the artificial. Knowing that the amberjack likes live bait near the surface, anglers hook or wire a baitfish to a short line on a stout rod and allow it to splash and flutter on the surface. The commotion is generally irresistible to prowling amberjack, and before long one of them will make a pass at the baitfish. The man on the teasing rod has to be quick, repeatedly taking the bait out of the water right in front of the gamester's open jaws. At the same time, he often swishes the rod tip in the water to create additional surface commotion.

At the end of the struggle, as it is being brought to gaff, a striped marlin "lights up" in a momentary color change. Billfish usually light up when they first sense the bait, giving anglers warning of the strike.

Amberjack have a short fuse, and it doesn't take long before their frustration leads to fury. A short, dark stripe runs through the eye of each amberjack, and the more excited this fish gets, the darker its stripes will become. The angler with the flyrod watches the stripe each time the fish makes a pass at the bait. When the color is dark enough to show the fish to be at the height of its annoyance, the teaser is pulled from the clear water and a large flyrod popper is dropped in its place. The amberjack hits that popper, and the fight is on.

Fear, too, may cause fish to change color rapidly. Perch, for example, can suddenly turn pale when frightened, the markings on their flanks standing out in bold relief.

CHANGING COLORATION

Color patterns often change throughout the life cycle of fishes. Fingerling salmons and trouts, with their infantile parr marks (dark side patches), look entirely different from the adults of the species. Fingerling largemouth bass are the color of the grass in which they hide (perhaps orange or yellow-brown) and have a stripe down their body that resembles a stalk of grass. In contrast, young smallmouth bass do not inhabit grass beds and do not have the longitudinal dark stripe down their sides because in open water it would be a giveaway rather than camouflage.

Bass, like many other game species, have the ability to change color to adapt to their surroundings. For example, they tend to become lighter over a lighter bottom and darker over a darker bottom. But the real masters of this art are the flounders, species that change their whole color pattern to match closely the details of the bottom they are on, whether it's shell, sand, gravel, grass, or anything else. The back of a flounder often looks like a photograph of the bottom.

Fish change colors in two ways. The slower method is a biochemical process in which the changes are controlled by the flow of chemicals through the blood. The faster method is through direct control whereby a signal is sent to the pigment cell via the nervous system telling it to open up and show color. This is precisely what happens in our example of a billfish about to strike a bait or an amberjack trying to capture a splashing baitfish. One thing is relatively certain: when the color in a fish changes rapidly, you know that it's excited and something is about to happen.

Professor F. B. Sumner designed some ingenious experiments based on color changes. His object was to prove that protective coloration was important to the survival of fish. To achieve this, he set up a dark-colored tank and a light-colored tank and then divided several thousand baitfish between the two tanks. The professor then waited six weeks until the fish had time to adjust their color to their surroundings. The fish in the dark tank gradually took on a darker hue and the fish in the lighter tank took on a lighter coloration.

At that point, he mixed his specimens so that both the dark tank and the light tank had half light and half dark fish. Then he turned some predatory penguins loose in each tank to see which fish they would catch more easily. As you might suspect, in the light tank the penguins took more of the dark "strangers" and in the dark tank they ate more of the light "strangers." Altogether the penguins caught nearly twice as many strangers (755 fish) as those that had adapted to the tank color (395 fish).

Dr. Sumner repeated the experiment using the night heron as the predator. Then, for the final test, he turned some green sunfish loose in the bait tanks. He was amazed to discover that the sunfish scored almost exactly the same as the birds. The sunfish accounted for just twice as many of the off-colored fish as those with the protective hue. Conditions were far from natural, but the experiments did show the survival advantage of a fish that is the same color as its background. Said another way, the test demonstrated scientifically the positive advantage of camouflage.

Inventive British anglers have adhered to this principle for years. They paint the inside of their minnow cans white so that the baitfish become a light color. Once these baits are on the hook and underwater, they contrast sharply with their darker surroundings and are much more visible to prowling perch and pike. The anglers claim that the number of strikes increases.

COLOR AND DEPTH

The results of nature's experiments with color are so complex and varied that it is not possible to develop a neat series of categories in which to place all fish according to their color patterns. But by taking some liberties of simplification, we can catalog a few color characteristics of fish. Perhaps the best way to get a broad look at the subject is to consider the offshore waters of the ocean where the maximum range of conditions exist. Here we notice a general correlation between color patterns and depth.

The bright surface layer is inhabited by fish and smaller life that are transparent or lightly colored with blue and green. At 500 feet, where the light is dimmer, the fish are gray or silver. At 1,000 feet they have brownish backs and silvery sides. Below 1,500 feet, where little light remains, fish and smaller life are black or red. Each of these colors provides a good deal of concealment at the depth where it prevails.

Therefore, in the deep ocean we can think of blue as a surface color; silver, gray, and brown as mid-depth colors; and red and black as deep-water colors. Yellow and orange are generally poor colors for concealment and are used mostly by fish that protect themselves in other ways, like the cave-dwelling reef fishes, so these colors are used sparingly in the open sea by nature, but lavishly on reefs and well-lighted shallow bottoms. Darker shades of orange and yellow would of course be concealing where the bottom growth has a yellow hue.

There are exceptions, however. Take the dolphin, brilliantly colored with yellows, browns, blues, and greens. The dolphin is a spectacular schooling gamester inhabiting the offshore surface waters in most of the tropical and temperate seas of the world. Our rule tells us that yellow is not the correct color for an open-water fish. Further investigation, however, would show that the dolphin is not quite an open-water fish. Although it prowls the seas, it likes to lurk around floating debris—rafts of yellow-brown sargassum weed, brown logs, gray hatch covers, and other flotsam and jetsam. So, its coloration does make sense.

In summary, we find that a solidly colored fish is by far the exception. Most species are countershaded to some degree, being dark on top and light underneath. Virtually all have some color markings no matter how faint or small. Strong camouflage patterns of disruptive coloration are typical of both bottomfish that live among rocks, grass, or rubble, and fish that live near the sunlit surface. Camouflaged bottomfish are generally characterized by full-color patterns over most of their body. Surface fish are more likely to have patterns only on the upper half. If a fish lives over a bottom that has vertical shadows from a weed bed, it is apt to have bars on its sides. A fish living over an irregular bottom will likely have patches of coloration. Spots and rings appear on fish in a variety of habitats, while stripes are found on fish that move between the bottom or mid-layers to the surface.

SEEING FISH UNDERWATER

Spotting a fish that is underwater takes practice and experience. The more you do it, the better you become. But like anything else, the skill doesn't come naturally and must be learned. It should be noted that you can spot fish underwater in fresh water as well as salt. Although some experienced observers can look into the water with naked eyes and see fish, most of us must use polarized sunglasses to help eliminate the glare, which is present even on an overcast day or when it is raining.

If possible, you should have the sun at your back so you can benefit from the penetrating rays. Think of the surface of the water as a window pane. The trick is to look right through it as if it weren't even there. It's like driving a car. You don't really see the windshield of your car, because you are concentrating on the road ahead. When you're spotting fish, you should be concentrating on the depths.

Altitude or height is also important. The higher you are above the water, the better you can see into it. An angler standing on the bow of a skiff can see better than his partner who is sitting down. A trout fisherman who carefully peers over a high bank can see better than another angler who is waist deep in the water.

Your eyes should scan the water, alert to any underwater movement. If you're moving along in a boat, even at a drift, the bottom is going to appear to be moving. You must learn to overlook the normal movement and concentrate on anything unusual. You might not see an outline of the entire fish as it would appear in a book, but be alert for a tail finning in the current or the head of a fish jutting out from behind cover.

Sometimes, the water isn't clear enough to see the fish well, but this is not the signal to relax. If you're fishing an artificial lure, you should be watching its progress, particularly as it nears the boat or the bank. Frequently, it's possible to see a gamefish following the lure, and you may want to work the artificial in a figure eight before lifting it from the water. Or there might be time to vary the retrieve. At least you know that you elicited a response from a fish and that can be an important factor in encouraging you to fish harder.

8

Feeding
Strategy

The number of fish of any species that reach old age is really minute when you consider how many start out as young. From the moment the eggs are spawned, the casualties begin. Some eggs are never fertilized. Others are eaten or destroyed before they can hatch. When the fry are hatched, they face a continuing struggle for existence through every phase of life. Every day, every month, and every year there are fewer and fewer representatives of that particular spawn still swimming about. A fish's survival is determined by its ability to feed successfully.

FEEDING AND GROWTH

To be successful at feeding and growing a fish must not only ingest enough food, but it must assimilate that food into its system with high efficiency. This means that the consumed food must be digested and passed in a dissolved state into the bloodstream where it provides nourishment to the fish's system. As food is assimilated and enters the bloodstream, it can be used in one of three ways. Most food is metabolized instantly to provide energy for immediate muscular activities or for internal purposes. Once this requirement is met, additional food is used to build muscle, bone, and body tissue as part of the growth process. Finally, some of the excess may be stored away for future use and this creates fat. But fat is only developed after the other conditions are met.

The task facing any fish is to locate, catch, and swallow its prey. Understanding feeding behavior, however, is not so simple.

Over the years, hundreds of scientific papers have been written on the feeding of fishes. In spite of reading each other's papers and debating the virtues of each theory at meetings, scientists still are unwilling to accept any single explanation of feeding behavior or of fish nutrition. Each specialist continues to favor his own views. This may sound like stubbornness, but science must have extensive proof. Obtaining this proof is not easy.

There is one point, however, on which the scientific community is in agreement about fish feeding: the key to success for an individual fish or an entire lake of fish is *efficiency*. Efficiency in feeding is a measure of how much food a fish can assimilate for a given amount of energy expended. This input-output ratio governs growth, vigor, and the day-to-day survival of every fish alive.

Feeding generally requires the greatest output of energy, but energy must also be used for spawning, migrations, and on a daily basis, for self-defense and for maintaining bodily functions. Fish that are forced to spend more energy in feeding than they can gain from the food they capture cannot keep up with their needs and eventually either die of starvation or are consumed by a predator in their weakened state.

As a general rule a fish must consume a minimum of 1 percent of its body weight each day in forage of average quality just to stay alive and active. On this basis, a 3-pound rainbow trout would have to ingest about a half ounce of food per day to have a minimum maintenance diet. In the course of a year, that rainbow trout would have to eat about 11½ pounds of food just to stay alive. All of the energy gleaned from that food would be used to capture it and to assimilate it. This rainbow trout, on a minimum diet, would probably be a long and slender fish.

Now suppose the trout were able to hunt down another 10 or 15 pounds of food. After all the extra feeding effort, it may gain a half pound of weight because so much of the food energy is needed to hunt down the prey. And the fish reaches a point where it must expend more energy in hunting than it gains from successful capture.

ENERGY TRADEOFFS

Anglers are continuously puzzled by the vagaries of feeding gamefish. For no apparent reason the fish will begin to feed voraciously, and then stop feeding and disappear. The fact is that fish exploit situations that give them the very best intake for a given amount of energy output. It is difficult for an angler to predict the consequences of the energy input-output scheme. But some explanation might help make fishing just a bit more successful.

Knowing that a fish automatically controls the output of energy, it stands to reason that a bait or lure should be placed where a fish can get it without great effort. And if you are imparting action or movement, the speed of trolling or retrieve (depending on the species you seek) should be at the minimum a fish will accept without hesitation. Try a slow retrieve first, and if you find that the fish are not interested, then speed up by steps until you begin to get strikes.

Some veteran largemouth bass fishermen have learned by long experience that the lunkers they seek are basically "lazy." On a retrieve they will work the lure for only 10 or 15 feet over the area where they suspect a bass is lying; then reel in and cast again to the target area. The odds are that a largemouth, unless it's very hungry, won't chase a lure more than a few feet. It just doesn't pay!

Engorging an entire baitfish in one gulp, a largemouth bass captures a nutritious meal without undue exertion. When feeding, fish must get the most nutrition for the least expenditure of energy.

As we see it, the problem is to get a fish to chase a bait or lure in the first place. Once the fish commits itself and gambles the initial burst of energy, it probably will continue the attack. If the fish does turn away without striking, there are two possibilities to consider: the offering may not seem worth an additional output of energy, or the presentation may have been unnatural. (The leader may be too heavy, retrieve too slow or too fast.)

FEEDING AND REST

It is natural to believe that fish can swim perpetually, and that they have the energy and speed to crash their prey for

A flash of silver on the Florida flats signals that a permit is on a hunting foray. Feeding primarily by sight, the permit must husband its strength and wait for the right moment to strike.

extended periods of time. Perhaps we would like to believe that every time a fish sees a potential meal it will run it down. Unfortunately, that's not the case. Because many anglers do not understand how fish feed, they suspect, when strikes are not forthcoming, that there are no fish in the lake or that they are using the wrong methods.

In general, feeding patterns and rest periods govern fish. Fish draw heavily on energy stores in feeding and must rest for many hours after each short burst of exertion. And because survival in the water is predicated upon the ability to escape pursuit, each fish must maintain reserve energy to escape predators waiting to take advantage of its fatigue.

If you've watched predators working over a school of baitfish, you know that the attacks are brief and seldom continue until all of the baitfish are destroyed. There are definite limits to a fish's exertions. J. R. Brett found that sockeye salmon took 3 hours and 12 minutes to recover from one period of moderate exercise during which they swam at 2 or 3 miles per hour until they were exhausted. According to a Washington research team, it takes steelhead 6 hours to recover from a similar experience. The same group found that individual coho salmon recover from fatigue in gradual stages. After one hour of rest, there is 31 percent recovery. Two hours of rest produce about 43 percent recovery, and after 3 hours, the fish are about two-thirds recovered.

The energy expended by salmon and trout moving upstream to spawn, often surmounting rapids and falls in their path, leaves them exhausted. Salmon fishermen, recognizing this, do most of their fishing around so-called "resting pools" where the fish can use deep water and rocks to minimize the current. If fish are moving upstream, you can generally find plenty of them in pools above and below an obstruction. Since swimming upstream is fatiguing, these fish must rest frequently. And in addition to the other reasons why spawning salmon don't take flies readily, one must consider their unwillingness to gamble energy at the moment.

In the fall of the year when the eastern brook trout is moving upstream to spawn, you frequently find the best fishing just above a set of rapids. Unlike the salmon, the brook trout will feed aggressively when it is in a spawning mood. A position at the head of the rapids enables it to rest as well as feed easily because natural food is being swept past its lie.

Experimenting with Kamloops trout, E. C. Black found that the top speed of yearlings dropped from 10 miles per hour to 2 miles per hour after only 3 minutes of strenuous swimming. The trout stayed in a school at first, but after 5 minutes they began to swim in different directions at irregular rates of speed. Black then tested their escape reactions and discovered that, when threatened, the fish escaped by rapid swimming at first. But after 5 minutes of exercise, these same trout tried to escape by hiding in dark corners of the raceway. The Kamloops trout required from 4 to 6 hours to recover from the fatigue of these swimming efforts.

Most stream fishermen, and especially those who prefer flyrods, usually play a fish gingerly. There is some realism in their argument about delicate leader tippets, but often they allow the fish to run downstream and then "dog it" by turning broadside to the current. When a fish turns broadside, you can't budge it with a light tippet, yet the fish isn't working that hard and can prolong the battle. If you are determined to beat a fish quickly, all you have to do is make it swim rapidly and keep swimming rapidly. After a few minutes, the fish will have lost most of its strength.

Physiologically, the energy for high-speed swimming comes from the glycogen stored in the muscles. The supply available, however, is extremely limited. As an example, the muscle glycogen supply of a rainbow trout is half used up in the first two minutes of heavy exertion. And once this store of energy is burned up, it takes more than twenty-four hours to build back to normal again. Consequently, a rainbow that has gone on a feeding spree or has broken your leader after a battle may have to spend a whole day or longer recuperating from the ordeal.

Fish that feed on plankton or bottom growth—the browsers—do not display the active attack strategies of the fish-eaters, nor do they feed in intensive bursts. Since these browsing fishes do not have to chase down their prey in sudden rushes, their patterns of energy use are different. They putter along for hours on end picking off plankton or rooting out bottom organisms with a steady energy output. And because they are not vigorous feeders, they are often not vigorous fighters once they are hooked.

If you're a trout fisherman, you may wonder how a trout can pick insects off the surface for a considerable period of time, seemingly without a rest. A trout chasing minnows can only feed for short periods of time. But trout that are nymphing or feeding on floating insects expend very little energy. The trout maintains a lie that affords protection from the

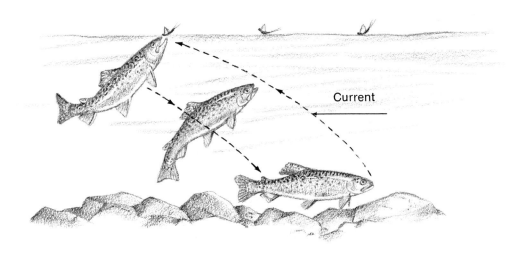

Current

Trout conserve energy when feeding on floating insects. From its hold-
ing position near the bottom, the trout sights the insect coming downstream, then lets the current carry it to the surface. Having taken the
fly, the trout sinks back to its lie.

current while enabling the fish to see the surface. As an insect
comes floating downstream, the trout seldom rushes forward
to grab it. Usually, it will let the current do all the work. The
fish starts to rise slowly, while the current carries it downstream. When the fish and fly intercept, the fish merely sucks
in the insect. Then it drops back toward the bottom and
calmly moves upstream to resume its lie.

Even if you can't see the fish underwater, you can generally assume that the lie of a trout is upstream from the point
where you saw the dimple on the surface. The key is to float
your own artificial along the same path as that taken by the
natural. It is also important to remember that it takes the fish
several seconds to resume a lie after rising, so hesitate a
moment before making the presentation.

In addition to using energy to hunt prey or merely to maintain position in a tide or current, trout and other fishes devote
a good deal of effort to protecting their feeding areas. Much
of this energy is spent driving away fish of their own species.

Above, a feeding trout breaks the still surface of a clear pool to suck in a mayfly. *Below,* bellies just touching bottom, two trout hold into the current by a protective rock, waiting for food to float by.

The black basses are never more aggressive than when they are defending their nests and their young, using up a great deal of energy in the process. The males protect their brood and the nest, fearlessly attacking any creature or object they believe might threaten the safety of their young.

For the whole breeding period of nearly a month, each mature male is fully occupied with defensive warfare. He drives other males away from his territory, females away from the nest, and attacks anything that wanders too close to the eggs or the school of fry. Although the largemouth bass will rarely feed during this period, he will strike at any lure that comes too close to his young. This trait makes him particularly vulnerable during the critical time.

THE LACTIC ACID PROBLEM

For many species fatigue leads to a serious physiological pitfall. Lactic acid builds up in the muscles during exercise periods and then naturally dissipates during rest when the blood rinses the muscles. In salmon and trout, lactic acid begins to accumulate in the bloodstream immediately after heavy exercise, building up to a peak in a few hours. From the time it starts to subside, twelve hours will elapse before the fish has regained a lactic-free state.

A fish can be killed outright by a high amount of lactic acid in the blood. Death probably occurs either because lactic acid stops the heart, or because it blocks the oxygenation of the blood by the gills. The research team of Parker, Black, and Larkin proved this effect on coho salmon more than ten years ago. Trolling off the British Columbia coast, they hooked and landed a considerable quantity of fish and placed their catch in live boxes aboard the boat. They studied the blood content of each fish and found that the lactic acid peaked in about three or four hours after it had been hooked. With the buildup of lactic acid, one fish died in the first hour, twenty-five in the second hour, fourteen more in the third hour, and nine more in the succeeding six hours. Nearly half of the cohos taken had died in the tanks during these tests.

The same team of scientists repeated their experiments with cohos that had left the ocean and were on their way upstream to spawn. This time, the results were completely different. The stream-caught fish did not die, even after total exhaustion from fighting on the hook. This led the scientists to conclude that the fish in the stream did not fight as hard as they did in open water; therefore, the lactic acid did not build up to such high proportions.

If you intend to kill your fish, the increase in lactic acid doesn't make any difference. But many fishermen today recognize the value of releasing at least a portion of their catch. In fact, a popular slogan among sportsmen today is "Limit your kill, don't kill your limit." Under these circumstances, the increase in lactic acid is a vital consideration. Fish that have been caught and released can and do survive. We have personally tagged thousands of bluefish, striped bass, and other gamefish, and we know that a good number of fish do survive after being caught on hook and line. Many of our tagging efforts have demonstrated a high percentage of recapture. But there has also been enough evidence of tagged fish washed up on shore, and loose tags, to prove that fish can die of fatigue.

ISOLATED OR DISABLED PREY

In his study of the feeding habits of rainbow trout in Paul's Lake, British Columbia, biologist E. J. Crossman reported that the older and larger rainbows raided schools of shiners when they gathered near the surface in the shallows. The trout attacked the shiners from below, creating a disturbance on the surface with each charge. Crossman emphasized that "In all cases observed, the trout appeared to be pursuing individual shiners rather than attempting to catch one at random by rushing through the center of the school." This is a key point in understanding the feeding of predatory fish: *Predators select and attack one specific victim at a time.*

Crossman also reported that there were usually from five to ten lone shiners lurking around the edges of the school, and that these isolated fish were far more vulnerable to predators than were those in the school itself. This illustrates another significant fact about predation: *Predators choose a victim that is isolated, disabled, or looks different.*

Packed tightly in a swiftly moving school, baitfish present a difficult target for a cruising predator. Seeing the school as a mass of shifting images, a predator usually singles out an isolated or disabled fish on the edge of the mass.

To the predator a tightly packed school of fish appears as a dense mass of shifting images rather than as a static formation of individual forms. Since most predators must select and attack one specific victim at a time to be successful, and because each fish in the school looks like every other one, it becomes nearly impossible for a predator to zero in on one fish. Thus an isolated fish at the edge of a school makes the best target. If an isolated fish is also disabled it stands out even more because of its irregular swimming and is easier for the predator to capture.

Among the thousands of predators, the fish that succeed are the ones that follow these rules of ignoring the school and picking a single prey that is isolated from the group. Each species has its own way of putting the rule into action. Some biologists believe that packs of predators often make blind charges into bait schools to panic their quarry. Then they whirl around and come back to pick off any confused or disoriented baitfish.

Knowing these principles it shouldn't be too hard to take some of those rainbows that were bombarding the shiners in Paul's Lake. Your best chances might be to disable a shiner, putting it on a hook, and casting it near the fringes of the school of baitfish. Or you could troll a shiner, or a lure that represented a shiner, around the fringes of the school.

While fishing for black marlin over Panama's Piñas Reef, we observed the two principles of predation in action. An acre of foraging bonito turned the surface into a froth over the reef, and we quickly caught a couple on handlines using feathers. The live bonito were sewn on hooks and streamed from the outriggers to spread them in the water. At the same time, the boat worked slowly along the fringes of the school of bonito. The effect was a disabled bonito that was somewhat isolated from its schoolmates. Black marlin hit that single bonito instead of feeding on a school that numbered thousands of fish.

Additional scientific observations confirm that predators seldom attack normal fish in a school, but prey instead off the weak, disoriented, or different-looking fish. In experiments with bowfin, Herting and Witt observed and measured this fact scientifically. They found that disabled bluegills, largemouths, and golden shiners were up to ten times more vulnerable than healthy ones of the same species.

SCHOOLING PREDATORS

Predators often school or attack in packs of a few fish to a dozen or so, to gain an efficiency on offense. With schooling or pack-hunting fishes, the group operates as a single unit; each member of the school benefits from the accumulated brains and tactical powers of all its members. In effect, the school becomes a single superfish.

Scientific discourse on why predators school fills up hundreds of pages in the literature about fish. One simple explanation is that a multi-point attack confuses the prey. A baitfish might easily dodge one predator, but with ten it wouldn't know which one had a bead on it. Also, predators derive an added benefit from disrupting a school of baitfish, for when baitfish panic and become disoriented they present more vulnerable targets. It is even better for the marauders when birds join the foray and crash into the water from above, causing additional panic and disorientation.

When three or four sailfish find a school of bait, they use a unique strategy based on their physical characteristics. Instead of trying to disrupt the school, they force it to pack even tighter. This is called "balling the bait." The sailfish swim around the bait with their dorsal fins (sails) extended. When the bait is packed into a tight ball, one fish at a time leaves the formation and slashes through the school with its bill, stunning several baitfish in the process. As the stunned bait struck by the bill start to settle, the fish makes another pass and swallows its meal. Then, it rejoins the circle and another fish moves in to feed. ·

The technique for hooking a sailfish under these circumstances is to stop the boat as the skipbait passes into the school of baitfish. It will start to settle and a sailfish should pick it up, believing he stunned it during the last raid. Other than that, it is very difficult to lure a sailfish away from the feast when the bait fish are balled up. The normal routine of moving a bait or lure out of the packed school won't work, because the sailfish, in this instance, is not interested in chasing stragglers but rather in disabling fish in the tightly packed school. At times, anglers can take sailfish by casting a dead bait into the pack. If you enjoy artificials, that's the time to let a fly settle in the school of baitfish or do the same thing with a shiny plug.

Even though predators often school up or form packs for feeding efficiency, frequently the largest specimens are loners. They will travel and feed by themselves or with another fish or two of similar size. Competition for food in the pack is keen

Like a single superfish, a school of predators—these are permit—can crash and destroy a school of baitfish in seconds. Confused by the multi-point attack, the baitfish are easy prey.

and the heavier fish aren't as agile as the smaller members of the pack. Thus, they can come out second best for the amount of energy expended and find it much more fruitful to hunt on their own.

FEEDING RHYTHM

Whether a species is a nighttime, daytime, or twilight feeder, there is a definite rhythm to its daily life. Many of its activities may be automatic so that the fish has no deliberate control over metabolic rate, eye adjustment, and even cruising speed. For example, bluefish swim constantly, never stopping to rest. But at night, they cease feeding and automatically

143

slow down to cruise at one-fifth of their daytime speed. Also, their eyes automatically begin to adjust for extra nighttime sensitivity even before dusk settles. The same advance tuning happens in the hours before dawn with a shift to the levels of swimming and eyesight needed for feeding in daytime.

Scientifically called circadian rhythm, this automatic behavior is probably present in all species of salt and freshwater gamefish that have periodic daily feeding peaks. The bluefish is a daytime feeder, the yellow perch a twilight feeder, the sole a nighttime feeder.

Researcher D. R. Swift found that the daily activity rhythm of brown trout was controlled automatically by light. He kept trout in submerged cages and electronically counted the number of times they swam by a sensing electrode. From late spring through early fall, the trout swam around five or ten times faster at noontime than at midnight. While most active they ingested the most food. The trouts' activity remained the same regardless of whether or not food was introduced. Swift interpreted this to mean that the activity pattern is not a response but rather an automatic function that the fish don't control, concluding from his experiments that the trout feeds because it is active, not that it is active in order to feed.

Ed Hobson, who has spent more than 1,200 hours underwater studying the feeding habits of dozens of species of shore fishes in the Gulf of California, reports that "a fine line exists between success and failure of attacks." He found that big predators had to work very hard for their daily meal, even over a reef area where there were herring, grunts, and other forage fish by the thousands. Feeding activity was governed by a very specific daily rhythm.

The complex battle plans for predators and the equally elaborate survival plans of prey are synchronized with the sun and based upon visual abilities. For example, herring migrate inshore and offshore each day. They go offshore at night to feed on plankton when the darkness provides safety from attack by the daylight predators. Most skirmishes occur during the transit period when the herring are moving in or out in the half-light of dawn and dusk.

AMBUSH FEEDERS

Many predators ambush their prey, an effective way to conserve energy and increase feeding efficiency. Some species hide in the rocks or grass until a victim swims by. Others hide behind a more innocent fish until they are within striking range of their target, while there are some who rely on their natural camouflage for concealment. J. B. Cott, expert on animal camouflage, explains that for any predator the "element of surprise at close range is everything."

The master of ambush is the muskellunge. In almost perfect camouflage, the muskie lies invisible among the weeds, patiently waiting for a potential quarry. As the victim approaches within striking distance, the muskie's muscles tense, it draws itself into an S-shaped form, and launches itself like a living torpedo, grabbing its prey crosswise between powerful jaws. It then turns the prey fish and swallows it head first by momentarily releasing its grip and shaking its head. Inexperienced fishermen using live bait for mus-

Predators such as the pike and muskie take a baitfish crosswise in their jaws, then turn it sideways before swallowing. The angler who strikes too soon will fail to hook his fish.

kies tend to set the hook too soon. Knowing that the fish will usually turn the bait, the best strategy is to give the quarry time to swallow its prey and then drive the barbs of the hook home. Their ability at ambush gives muskies a wide range of prey, including turtles, muskrats, minks, rats, gophers, squirrels, ducklings, and songbirds.

The northern pike, a close relative of the muskie, has a different feeding plan. Pike don't really hide, but depend strictly on the concealing effect of their camouflage color pattern to give them the element of surprise at close range. They stay at the edge of weedbeds or near the bottom in open water, relaxed, with their tails drooping down. When a pike senses the presence of prey, the dorsal fin snaps up, both dorsal and anal fins begin to pulse rhythmically, and the front two-thirds of the body stiffens as it rises from the bottom and begins to stalk the prey with a screwlike movement of the tail. When the distance, target angle, and position are exactly perfect, it launches a straight-line attack, grasps its prey crosswise, turns it, and gulps it down.

Down through the centuries, pike have perpetuated their reputation as an evil spirit of the waters. With their prominent teeth and generally threatening appearance, pike are well cast in their role. According to icthyologist Keen Buss, "Pike existed in medieval literature simply to attack swans, men, and even mules. Mystery, of course, has always been an important ingredient in angling, and nothing stirs the soul more than the abrupt arrival of a 20-pound pike behind the lure. With baleful eyes and underslung jaw, it comes grimly to the feast."

TOOTHY FEEDERS

Pike and muskellunge are daytime feeders that hunt strictly by sight, like their saltwater counterpart, the barracuda. The 'cuda, which usually relies on speed and strength to catch its prey, often hangs suspended in the water, barely moving a fin until its prey comes within range.

J. Randall, an expert scientific observer, reports that the typical attack of a large barracuda on a cero mackerel is a swift lunge, a chop to sever the victim in half, and a leisurely return to swallow the chunks. Barracuda, may also swallow baits whole, tail first, head first, or folded in the middle.

Barracuda have the nasty habit of responding to vibrations sent out by a hooked fish, and anglers are sometimes frustrated by the 'cuda's habit of chopping a hooked fish in half. According to B. Halstead, an expert on dangerous fish, a 'cuda will cut a fish as if it had been chopped with a meat cleaver. The slice is straight and clean with no ragged edges. A shark, on the other hand, will tear the fish by shaking its head once the jaws have clamped down, instead of biting cleanly. The bite is curved with jagged edges conforming to the shape of the shark's jaws.

The bluefish has such a reputation for chopping bait that it is commonly nicknamed the "chopper" along the northern Atlantic Coast. It has been called "perhaps the most ferocious and bloodthirsty fish in the sea, leaving in its wake a trail of dead and mangled mackerel, menhaden, herring, alewives, and other species upon which it preys."

King mackerel also chop their prey at times. There's hardly an angler familiar with the king who hasn't marveled at this fish's uncanny ability to chop a bait within a fraction of an inch of the hook. Experienced fishermen generally rig a bait with a tandem hook, and the back hook is invariably the one that takes the fish. A close relative, the cero mackerel, often makes long, low, graceful leaps into schools of herring, balao, silversides, and other baitfish, an apparent attempt to gain elevation for an attack from above.

CAUTIOUS FEEDERS

At the other extreme, there are fish that exhibit very cautious feeding habits, testing the mettle of the most polished angler. Some bottom species are notorious bait stealers and can "mouth" a bait off the hook without an angler realizing it. As a countermeasure, learn the habits of these fish and set your own reactions accordingly.

When worm fishing for trout, you may feel a strike yet keep missing when you try to set the hook. Francis Ward, who watched trout feeding for long periods, offers this explanation: "Unless trout are exceedingly hungry, I do not believe they ever swallow a worm until they have killed it. They may bite it and spit it out two or three times successively . . . or taking it in their mouths, they masticate it well for several minutes before trying to swallow it."

The winter flounder is well-known among Atlantic saltwater fish for its delicate eating habits. Instead of chewing their food, the flounder suck it in slowly (they have very small mouths), move off, and swallow it as they go. If they feel the hook or resistance from the sinker, they frequently disgorge the bait.

Techniques for flounder run from using a chum pot to pushing a household plunger mounted on a long pole into the soft mud bottom to stir up natural foods. The mainstay of the flounder's diet in many estuaries is the clam neck. Flounder pull the yellowish tip off the neck of the clam where it protrudes above the bottom. We have opened flounder from New Jersey bays with thirty or forty clam tips in their stomachs. Because the softshell clam can regenerate a new tip three or four times in its life, each clam can furnish that number of meals for a flounder. Clams are currently prospering in our sewer-rich bays (pollution prevents people from eating them), creating an abundant food source for the clam-eating flounder (which is one of the few coastal fishes that is prospering these days). A clam tip looks just like a kernel of canned corn. An irresistible chum for flounder can be made by mixing corn with a few clam tips to give off an odor. Bait up with a clam or worm and you should do exceptionally well.

FEEDING SHYNESS

In a comprehensive series of tests, it was demonstrated that largemouth bass were very quick to learn they should avoid hooks. And once bass do learn about hooks, they remain hook-shy for six months according to scientists Anderson and Heman who did the experiments. The researchers conditioned their bass in two experimental lots, one that was heavily fished (100 hours per acre) and one that was left in the virgin state. For the experiments, the bass were sorted out by size, the "fished" and "virgin" groups were identified by different fin clips, and then they were both fished under carefully controlled conditions using artificial lures. None of the fish caught were returned to the ponds.

Anderson and Heman found that in the 9- to 12-inch group of fish, four times as many virgin bass (those that had never been fished before) were taken. Forty percent of the virgin bass were caught out of the pond, but only 10 percent of the "fished before" group succumbed to an artificial lure. For bass 12 inches and larger, the results were even more convincing, with five times as many virgin bass being taken. Differences for fish under 9 inches were not significant, and the researchers believe this may have been due to an experimental defect. It also may be that young fish don't learn as fast.

Completely separate lots of fished and virgin bass were tagged and kept in another lake until the following spring to see if the fished group would retain its hook shyness for as long as six months. During the first two weeks of the spring fishing season, the "experienced" group still resisted capture by three to one. In the second two-week period, the ratio dropped to three to two. Presumably the virgin fish were learning hook avoidance. Anderson and Heman believe that the bass which saw their schoolmates caught learned the danger of the hook *by example, not* by being hooked themselves. Anderson and Heman cited other experiments where fingerling bass learned to avoid worms with hooks in them while hungrily devouring free worms. But we believe that in any stock of gamefish there are, at any time, fish that are naturally vulnerable and those that are naturally hook-shy. Learning is not involved, just simply a natural difference in "intelligence." Some fish are basically more clever than others in resisting a lure or a baited hook. Consequently, the angler usually catches the "dumber" fish, leaving the more clever ones behind. A stock of hook-shy fish remains and it becomes more and more difficult to hook one of them as time goes on because the vulnerable ones are rapidly being caught.

The typical experience of most fishermen is to find that the good fishing of opening day rapidly gives out. And in a few days or weeks, the fish become increasingly difficult to hook. One might assume that this is all due to scarcity, but hook shyness is primarily responsible.

George Bennett's work with bass at Ridge Lake, Illinois, confirms this theory. He showed that 20 to 50 man-hours of fishing per acre on opening day was enough to substantially reduce the rate of catch for largemouth bass. Bennett figures that limiting the amount of fishing to something below two men per acre per day is necessary to prevent the effects of hook shyness in a bass lake. Bennett calls the effect "wariness," and because he notes a return to vulnerability after the fall and winter resting period, he believes the condition to be temporary rather than a permanent characteristic of the hook-shy fish. Even with this apparent resiliency, we believe there is a permanent natural tendency for some fish to be more clever about hook avoidance than others.

In any population of gamefish, there are some specimens that are naturally resistant to being caught by a *particular* type of lure. Someone could come along with a new or different type of lure and do exceptionally well. The vulnerable fish have already been caught and there remains a hard core that are resistant to all current lures, but might be vulnerable to a certain new lure that appears on the scene. This new "killer" may prove to last in effectiveness only until the newly vulnerable fish are caught. Anglers frequently wonder why last year's "killer" lure has lost its effectiveness, while other artificial lures are successful year after year. For one thing, the lure in question can represent a particular type of bait that is no longer present in an area for one reason or another. Or it may have been so effective on the vulnerable portion of the stock as to take nearly all of them.

The lures that do endure and continue to produce fish possess what scientists call a "releaser." There is something about them that causes the fish to attack. It could be the "flash" or possibly a spot behind the "gill cover." Perhaps it is the action, but whatever it is, there is a releaser present that triggers the response from a gamefish.

We also contend that part of the answer to why certain lures only prove effective for a short time lies in genetics. The fish that are best adapted to survive (including those who have a resistance to fishermen's baits and lures) live to spawn and pass their resistance along to future generations. The weak and the vulnerable perish and do not pass these traits along to the next generation. Any weakness would apply. Thus the fish of a genetic strain that are vulnerable to a new killer lure are caught up rapidly and the survivors are those that don't succumb to the temptation of the lure. The resistant fish make up most of the spawning stock and most of the young will probably also exhibit a resistance to the lure in question. This takes a varying number of years depending upon how fast the fish become mature spawners, how long it takes the new fingerling to reach catchable size, and upon several other factors. But in many cases, the effect could be obvious in two or three years. That, in part, could explain why a lure that was extremely successful for a few years suddenly fails to produce fish.

PREPARING THE HOOK

Many anglers are careless about the condition of the hooks they use. Even those who sharpen single hooks seldom take the time to sharpen treble hooks. Some fish have soft mouths and it's relatively easy to drive the barb home. However, if the point of the hook should hit bone or cartilage, or the fish has a hard mouth, penetration can be difficult. To achieve rapid penetration, even a hook that has just been taken out of a new box requires sharpening.

A hook should possess cutting edges. A hypodermic needle, for example, is not solely a sharp-pointed instrument; the edges are razor-sharp to cut through the skin. Triangulation of a hook is one way of obtaining cutting edges. It can be done quickly with a hook hone or a fine file by forming two or three cutting edges between the point and the barb. Picture an imaginary line on the side of the point opposite the barb. The first step is to flatten this side. Then work inside the bend of the hook filing from each of the two corners created by the flat side toward the center. You'll end up with a triangular point and the hook will penetrate much more easily.

SETTING THE HOOK

If you're fishing with bait, the hook is often concealed inside the offering, but the point should protrude just enough so that when you set the hook, it will cut through the bait and extend in a position where it can hook the fish. There's a tendency among fishermen to set a hook by rearing back on the rod. This one long pull seldom does the job, which is to drive the point of the hook into the mouth of the fish past the barb. The best way to do this is to keep the rod in front of you and lift in a series of four or five short, sharp, upward jerks. The rod doesn't have to move through a very wide arc to accomplish this.

Before you set the hook on any fish, the line between the rod tip and the fish must be perfectly tight. Slack prevents the action of the rod from being transmitted to the hook. Reel up all slack first or wait until the fish pulls the slack line tight and then set the hook.

Any strike on an artificial is a direct take—that is, the fish intends to swallow it directly. You can bet that the fish isn't about to hold the lure in its mouth, play with it, and then swallow it. Your quarry will quickly realize that it's not the genuine article and expel it. Yet, it takes longer for this to happen than you might suspect.

When a fish opens his mouth to hit any bait or lure, he is also swallowing water. In fact, the bait really floats into his mouth and it will continue to float while the water is being expelled through the gills. Usually, a fish won't detect an artificial until he has ejected the water and clamps down on it.

When a fish takes a lure, it also takes in water *(top)*. Lure floats in mouth until water is expelled through gills *(bottom)*. Most anglers set the hook too soon, when lure is still floating in the mouth.

▶

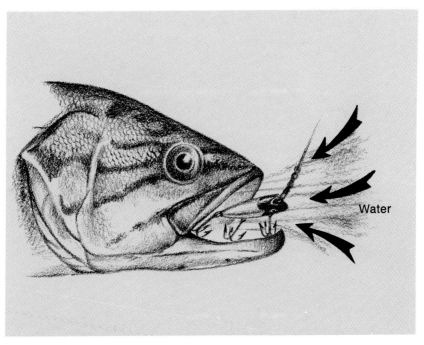

Water

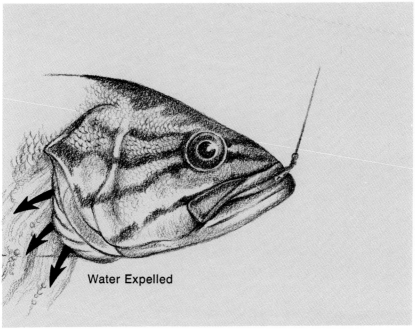

Water Expelled

Striped bass hooked firmly on an artificial lure. Learning when to set the hook on a fish takes a sensitive touch—and lots of experience.

The common failing among fishermen using artificials is to set the hook too soon. Of course, it depends on the type of fishing. A trout, for example, can take a fly or a nymph and reject it almost as quickly as you can read this. But there are fish of many species that take considerably longer to make up their minds. Don't misunderstand and believe that you have unlimited time, but you do have much more than you would suspect. For many species, it is critical to wait until the fish takes the lure and turns before trying to set the hook. This is particularly true when you can see what is happening. If you do set too soon, the artificial is usually floating in a mouthful of water, and when you raise the rod tip, the lure merely floats out of the mouth. Learning when to set the hook is an art and there's no substitute for practical experience. As a rule of thumb, if you feel resistance when you set the hook but you don't hook the fish, possibly you're setting too soon. On the other hand, if everything is limp at the time you set, the fish probably already rejected the offering. Plugs with two or three sets of treble hooks don't offer any advantage in hooking a fish. It's really easier to hook and hold a fish with a single set of trebles or a single hook.

The double take—when a fish grabs the prey and mouths it—occurs primarily with natural bait and especially with live bait. Fishing live bait properly takes a great deal of skill. Beginners tend to pull the bait out of the fish's mouth by setting too soon. In most instances, the correct procedure is to let the fish grab the offering. Point the rod tip directly at the fish and keep the reel in free spool or with the bail in the open position. The idea is to minimize the amount of pressure so that the fish won't suspect the bait isn't the real thing.

Very often, the gamefish will grab the bait and move off with it. Then he'll stop, turn it around, play with it, or kill it before swallowing it. You should allow time for these contingencies. In many cases, when the fish has swallowed the bait, it will start to move off again and that's the time to set the hook. In time, you develop a sensitivity for knowing what's happening even though you can't see it. On some species you learn to set the hook sooner than you would on others.

The technique of hooking a fish has been refined further to compensate for the angle at which a fish strikes in relation to the angler. This works best where you can see the actual attack. If, for example, a fish is moving from right to left (at right angles to the fisherman), the angler has the option of setting the hook by lifting the rod or by sweeping the rod sideways. Either way, the hook should hit the corner of the mouth. The best angle is when the predator strikes the prey while moving directly away from the angler. Then there's every chance that the hook will find flesh as it's pulled back toward the mouth by the action of the rod.

The most difficult angle is the head-on take, when a fish is coming directly at you. The tendency is to pull the offering out of its mouth. If you can, let the fish grab the bait or lure and then wait until he turns before you strike. If you can't wait, sweep the rod sideways instead of straight up and try to drive the barb into the corner of the mouth.

9

Food Selection and Nutrition

As a rule, fish are extremely selective about their diets. At times they may adopt a wider diet than normal as a matter of survival, but usually they won't vary extensively in their choice of food. Each fish picks and chooses from the available supply of food, selecting those same items the species has preferred for thousands of years.

Predators feed most efficiently when they are highly selective. They regularly change their choice of prey to take advantage of a temporary abundance of food, such as a hatch of mayflies or a migration of bait. Off the coast of South Africa, for example, a host of predators will follow the annual migration of sardines for a thousand miles or more. The bluefish of our own East Coast arrive in late spring on the heels of the mackerel migration. Coho in the Great Lakes tail the huge schools of alewives. Trout in rivers move upstream to take advantage of progressive insect hatches.

Extensive studies of the feeding patterns of brown trout revealed that the fish put on almost 65 percent of their total year's growth during the few weeks of heavy feeding that accompanies the insect hatches in the spring. In January, the same fish will feed on stone-fly nymphs almost exclusively, but digestion is a slow process in the colder water temperatures of winter and growth at that time of year is minimal.

Some scientists are convinced that trout feed selectively for the purpose of gaining efficiency. They reason that the value of selective feeding may be that the trout uses its energy more economically by repeating the same movement to snap up larvae instead of changing its feeding movements for different kinds of food. We believe this is the basis of food selection among fish and probably explains why they frequently feed exclusively on one prey for extended periods of time, often ignoring everything else. A classic example occurs when a trout is nymphing—that is, taking nymphs right under the surface of the water. As the trout rolls, his tail breaks water and it appears as if he were taking mayflies. Many fishermen are fooled by this and spend frustrating moments trying to match the hatch with a dry fly.

To gain an insight into the food preferences of fish, scientists observed the feeding patterns of species in several Ontario lakes. They discovered that yellow pickerel ate a variety of foods, but their diet averaged 48 percent fish, 28 percent insects, and 23 percent crayfish. At the same time and in the same lakes, northern pike balanced their diet with 45 percent fish and 53 percent crayfish, completely ignoring the insects. Smallmouth bass in those waters were eating only 25 percent fish and 75 percent crayfish, while the garpike limited their diet to nearly 100 percent fish.

An angler fishing these waters would no doubt do best if he fished a crayfish for smallmouths or northerns; there's a good chance he would take yellow pickerel on the same bait. If his goal were strictly pickerel or northerns, live minnows would be a good choice. Smallmouths as a rule may prefer crayfish to minnows, but if a smallmouth resides in a body of water that does not support an extensive crayfish population, he will probably switch to a heavier diet of minnows and anglers would do best fishing live minnows or minnow-type artificials.

A Minnesota research team led by W. M. Lewis confirmed the preference of bass for crayfish during experiments conducted in experimental ponds. During a 20-day series of tests, the bass were offered 1,000 crayfish and 1,000 bluegills. They consistently took crayfish in preference to fish at the amazing ratio of 24 crayfish for every bluegill.

The team then ran additional tests and found that the bass gained weight when they ate crayfish and black bullheads, but they actually lost weight on bluegills and green sunfish. Tadpoles also turned out to be a favorite food, but in spite of the quantity eaten, the bass were only able to maintain their present weight without gaining.

Philip W. Smith and Lawrence M. Page studied the feeding of spotted bass in Illinois' Wabash River and came up with the following percentage diets:

Type of Food	Size of Bass		
	1-3 inches	3-6 inches	6-12 inches
Plankton	41%	—	—
Aquatic insects	82	75%	48%
Terrestrial insects	12	25	30
Crayfish	3	15	39
Other arthropods (water fleas, spiders)	9	20	3
Fish	3	40	33
Miscellaneous	3	—	6

A study in Ontario by W. E. Ricker showed that smaller brook trout of 10 to 11 inches had an average of 1/14 ounce of food in their stomachs, while the larger ones of 11 to 16 inches had 1/5 to 1/6 of an ounce. To gain the extra food they needed as they grew larger, the brookies gradually shifted over from a fare of insects to fish and crayfish.

Extensive studies of smallmouth bass in Ontario lakes showed that these bass made the first shift from tiny morsels to larger fare when they were very young. Fingerling smallmouth started out on plankton and then changed to insects. But when they were 2 inches long, they switched to a diet mainly of fish. After they reached 3 inches in length they switched again. This time they concentrated on crayfish. And when they grew a little larger, their eating habits permanently changed back to fish as the major item in their diet. Among all sizes of bass recorded in the sample, the average diet consisted of 28 percent fish (perch, minnows, etc.) and 72 percent small crayfish. And as indicated, the largest bass ate almost 100 percent fish.

One would expect selection to be strongly influenced by the relative abundance of crayfish and fish in the particular lake investigated. Interestingly enough, the Ontario study found the fattest and most robust smallmouths in Lake Nipissing, where the diet consisted of 80 percent crayfish. In fact, similar studies in Perch Lake, where the bass ate only 40 percent crayfish, showed them to be leaner than in Lake Nipissing. This suggests, of course, that smallmouths seem to do better on crayfish. They can hunt fish for food, but they seem to lose efficiency in the tradeoff as compared to hunting crayfish. From this analysis, it would stand to reason that a lake with a large natural supply of crayfish would support a substantial bass population, and the bass, on an average, should grow faster in that lake.

Both brown and rainbow trout shift to a primary diet of fish as they get older and larger. The shift occurs rather suddenly at a size somewhere between 9 and 12 inches. The purpose of this change in diet is to improve feeding efficiency —that is, to increase food intake for a given output of energy.

A research project in Paul Lake, British Columbia, demonstrated that this strategy succeeds for the fish. The rainbow trout studied had twice as much food in their stomachs if they were feeding on fish (shiners) than if they were feeding on lower forms (insects)—1/7 of an ounce compared to 1/14 of an ounce. The change in feeding habits took place when the fish reached about 10 inches in length. During the summer months, rainbows less than 10 inches ate only 6 percent shiners on an average, while those from 10 to 14 inches ate 79 percent shiners, and those larger than 14 inches included 94 percent shiners in their diet.

From the foregoing, it is easy to understand why it is extremely difficult to coax large trout into taking a dry fly. Certainly they are caught in this manner, but the percentages are against it happening with any marked frequency because of their basic preference for fish.

If you are able to determine the specific prey on which a fish is feeding (and this may last for days or only a couple of hours), the best approach is to use a bait of the approximate size. If that doesn't work, use something larger. The next time you catch a trout that has been feeding on insects, dissect the stomach carefully. Frequently, you'll be able to see distinct layers of different insects. Even though they were all eaten within the span of a few hours, the types are carefully separated in the stomach because of the fish's tendency to specialize. As one type of insect became scarce, the trout switched abruptly to another type.

During a specific hatch, you should make every attempt to match the size, basic coloration (dark or light), and the silhouette of the natural insect. A tiny collection net carried on your fly vest is an excellent tool for culling insect samples from the surface of the water. If you believe that a trout is nymphing, try to discover the size and coloration of the nymph. You may know this if you can identify hatching insects. Otherwise, the alternative is to locate typical nymphs in the stream and then use your judgment.

East Coast striped-bass buffs know that the preferences of the bass vary at different times of the year depending on the available food supply, and they use this knowledge to their advantage. A good bass angler usually has a fairly good idea of what's in the stomach of every fish he catches. If stripers are gorging on calico crabs, he'll bait up with a calico. If they are picking off herring at a stream mouth, he'll swim a live herring out to them. At night, he may live-line an eel, because stripers simply can't resist that slithery creature. Recently, swimming live bunkers (menhaden) in a tide rip has paid off handsomely. Live mackerel also work wonders when schools of them are flooding the coastline.

SIZE OF PREY

The Russian expert on fish feeding, I.V. Ivlev, has advanced the principle that *if a predator has a choice, it will select the largest size prey it can handle easily.*

In comparison to their own length, young predators often take prey that is extremely large. Biologists have concluded that, on the average, the smallest predators take prey that range from 40 to 50 percent of their own length. Sport fishermen have often observed this when they manage to hook a fish that is not much longer than their lure.

Full-grown predators tend to favor prey that is only 10 to 20 percent of their own length. To ingest the same percentage of food in relation to size, larger fish would have to hunt down and capture far more prey than smaller fish. Yet most scientists have noted that large fish don't expend the energy to catch a volume of prey proportionate to their weight, and that is one of the reasons that they grow more slowly.

G. H. Lawler, a specialist on feeding, found the following relationship between the size of pike and the most common size of their prey:

Length of Pike	Length of Sucker Eaten	Length of Perch Eaten
10″	4″	4″
15″	5″	4½″
20″	5½″	5″
25″	8½″	8″
30″	9½″	—

It's interesting to note that the perch were always slightly smaller than the suckers and one could easily theorize that pike allowed a little leeway for the spiny-rayed dorsal of the perch.

In one study, the size of the stomach opening of bass (the esophagus) was measured and compared to the girth of their

Ready to engulf a prey, a rock bass opens its mouth amazingly wide. Fish always can judge whether they can handle a prey, usually select the largest available.

prey. It was found that bass would usually select prey that were somewhat smaller than the maximum opening of their stomachs.

Fish have the ability to instantly judge the size of their prey. Underestimating the girth of its prey could be fatal to a fish. The prey would probably get stuck halfway down the esophagus, and spines on the dorsal fin would prevent the predator from regurgitating its victim, resulting in starvation, suffocation, damage to the gills, or exhaustion.

HOW MUCH DO FISH EAT?

Predatory gamefish consume amazing amounts of baitfish in a season's feeding, even though much of it might be in spurts. Biologist E. D. Toner, after careful consideration, concluded that 1,170 pike living in one Irish lake ate 46 tons of brown trout each year. Scientists also estimated that 100 walleyes, such as might occupy a few miles of an Illinois river, would consume 180,000 to 300,000 baitfish of 3 to 4 inches in length during their average life span of three years.

Just to stay alive and healthy, a predatory fish must eat an amount of food each day equal to 1 percent of its body weight. A 3-pound largemouth would have to ingest at least a half-dozen small minnows or crayfish to get this minimum daily requirement. But to grow normally, the same bass would need 2 to 3 percent of its body weight per day, and to accomplish this, it would have to come up with somewhere between 12 and 23 minnows and crayfish.

The total food that a bass can consume in one day is limited by the size of its stomach and its rate of digestion. Experiments show that with an abundant supply of favored food available—crayfish, tadpoles, shiners—a bass could eat and digest a maximum of 12 percent of its body weight per day. To accomplish this peak rate of feeding, the experimental bass ate 30 golden shiners and 40 tadpoles apiece over a 10-day period, or a little over 2 pounds of food each. And the food was supplied for the fish. In natural surroundings, finding and capturing this quantity of food is a very difficult task.

For bluegills and similar panfish, the maximum intake appears to be 3 or 4 percent of body weight per day, with a normal intake of 1 or 2 percent. Carp are known to eat as much as 16 percent of their body weight per day during periods of peak feeding.

HIBERNATION

Winter is a time of hibernation or semi-hibernation for many species. About the latter part of November or early December, depending upon the latitude, smallmouth bass, for example, cease feeding entirely and are usually seen no more until about March or early April, after the ice is gone. A water temperature of about 50 degrees Fahrenheit marks the beginning and the end of activity. In southern waters, of course, they may continue to feed all year.

In the North, a smallmouth will hibernate like a bear, finding a cave in the rocks or a hollow in a tree stump. And it may have company, because when they are not feeding, bass stop fighting about territory and get quite chummy. The story is often told about a man named Seth Whipple, who lived on the Hudson River near Glen Falls. In drawing some sunken logs from the river during the winter for firewood, he found in the hollow of one of the logs six smallmouth bass weighing from ½ to 2 pounds. There are many other accounts of bass hiding in rocky caves, crevices, or piles of driftwood.

Tautog, an ocean species, are also known to hibernate whenever they can find cover offshore, perhaps in the hull of a sunken ship or barge. Hibernating inshore is not safe along the northern seaboard because in the winter, estuarine and inshore waters are too cold. Sea temperatures can fall to 28 degrees F. because of the antifreeze effect of the salt in ocean water. Fresh water, of course, can only drop to 32 degrees F. before it freezes.

However, any temperature below 30.5 degrees F. is dangerous to ocean-adapted fish since that is the freezing point of their blood and tissues. This is probably the reason that striped bass along the northeastern coast move well up into tidal rivers to hibernate, where the water is fresh enough to remain above the lethal point of 30.5 degrees F. Stripers lie semidormant at an intermediate depth or in holes in the bottom. Resident fishes that winter in estuaries have antifreeze chemicals in their body fluids. But the strategy for most coastal species is to migrate south in the winter to warmer offshore waters.

In fresh water, many species do remain active and feeding throughout the winter months, providing excellent sport for anglers who enjoy fishing through the ice. Ice fishermen account for excellent catches of trout, pike, salmon, walleye, and a number of panfish. Biologists W. E. Frost and M. E. Brown report in their book *The Trout* that they have found brown trout with full stomachs in water of 37 degrees F. In Ireland, half of the trout caught in November, December, and January had stomachs that were three-quarters full of food, due to the slow rate of digestion in winter.

DIGESTION

Fish of all species usually require at least twelve hours to digest their food under the best conditions. Since digestion is a chemical process, the rate of the process is a function of body temperature. Because fish are cold-blooded, their bodies and body chemicals are at nearly the same temperature as the surrounding water. Therefore, in winter, digestion is slowest and in the summer it is fastest.

When the water temperature ranges from 70 to 77 degrees, largemouth bass digest the food in their stomachs in about eighteen hours. But in winter, the same bass would take four days or longer to digest their food. And the rates are exactly the same for smallmouth.

The various sunfishes—bluegills, crappies, pumpkinseed—digest food at about the same rate as the black basses to which they are so closely related. These sunfishes require about three-quarters of a day to digest food in summer and four days or longer in winter. Perch and pike digest the food in their stomachs in one day during the summer when water temperatures range from 68 to 77 degrees, two days in spring and fall when temperatures are 46 to 57 degrees and nine days in winter at temperatures around the freezing point.

The digestion rates of saltwater species are also controlled by temperature. Sole digest in fourteen to eighteen hours at about 60 degrees, at which temperature black bass would require twenty-four to thirty-six hours. Sole are nocturnal feeders and usually have three-quarters of the night's meal in their stomach by noon the following day, but only 5 percent remains by five o'clock that same afternoon.

On certain aspects of digestion, scientists have failed to come up with a unanimous opinion. For bass and bluegills, researcher J. T. Windell showed that large meals are digested as rapidly as small ones. He also proved that larger sizes of prey are digested as fast as smaller ones. Furthermore, both bluegills and bass digested different types of prey—insects, crayfish, fish—at about equal rates of speed.

Windell also found that starvation greatly *decreases* the digestive power of fish. In experiments, bluegills were starved for various periods; when they were fed again, those starved for twenty-five days could digest only half as fast as normal fish. It took about six days after feeding started again before digestion was back to a normal rate.

In the winter, nutrition is slowed down by reduced feeding activity and lower food intake in addition to the slower digestion. Bass, for example, may consume less than one-tenth of their summer rations yet still survive the winter because in their state of hibernation and low activity they use up very small amounts of energy. Species such as Arctic char that inhabit frigid waters and only have a short growing season, add weight and size at a very slow rate.

For many fishes, the threat of starvation in winter is very real. Fortunately, most fish have an amazing ability to go for long periods of time without food, recovering quickly once food is available again. British biologist R. M. Love showed that it takes seventy-eight days to starve a cod to death, even at a temperature of 57 degrees, which is exceptionally warm for cod and should speed the process greatly. Russian researchers carried fingerlings of many species to the death point to see what rates of starvation they could find at temperatures between 64 and 79 degrees Fahrenheit. In order to get a fair average, they computed the time that it took for 90 percent of the fingerlings studied to succumb. It took thirty days for herring, forty days for perch, fifty-five days for sturgeon, seventy-five days for pike, sixty-five days for carp. All of the species lost between 30 and 35 percent of their body weight by the time of death.

ASSIMILATION OF FOOD

A fish is not truly a successful feeder unless a high percentage of the food it devours is assimilated by its system and chemically converted so it can be utilized for energy and growth. Species differ in their ability to assimilate food. As an example, experiments show the rate of protein utilization declines with age. In studies with bluegills, it was found that two-year-old fish assimilated or actually utilized 35 percent of the protein they swallowed. Eight-year-old fish only assimilated

Sunfish in this lake compete with other panfish for food. They are also prey of larger fish such as bass and pike. Panfish like these consume up to 4 percent of their body weight per day during peak feeding periods.

20 percent. Thus, as a fish gets older, it benefits from a little over half as much usable protein as younger fish do. This lower rate of protein assimilation certainly reduces the growth potential in the older fish. True growth, by the way, is the addition of new flesh and bones and does not include the storage of fat.

Considering all elements of food—carbohydrates, fats, and protein—older fish appear to be quite inefficient. On the average, they utilize only 15 percent of what they consume, while the younger fish assimilate about 45 percent of their intake. That's why early growth is so much more rapid and why it takes much more food for an already large fish to get larger. Consequently, hatchery men are faced with a double problem in trying to grow trout to a large size. First, older fish eat far less in proportion to their body weight, and second, they utilize what they do eat very ineffectively. A standard hatchery ration for maximum growth efficiency of brook trout, browns, and rainbows is 6 percent of the body weight per day for 4- to 5-inch fish and only 2 percent for 9- and 10-inch fish.

Appetite is also a controlling factor in the efficiency of nutrition among fishes. In experiments with brown trout and northern pike, scientists discovered that hungry fish assimilated food better than those that were already well fed. In fact, it seems that an optimum rate of assimilation occurs at a point that is far less than the total amount that the fish would normally eat.

As a broad generalization, fish convert the food consumed into additional weight at a ratio varying from 10 to 20 percent. That is, 1 pound out of every 5 to 10 pounds of food eaten is assimilated for growth. The remainder of the food intake is burned up in normal energy used for swimming, feeding, migrations, reproduction, and similar functions. In a study of pike in the Volga River, 1 pound of weight was added for every 8.8 pounds of food consumed. Since younger pike are more efficient and can convert food to growth at a higher rate, they gained 1 pound for every 3 to 5 pounds of food ingested. However, it still took 700 small perch to grow a pike to 1 pound.

So when you are successful in landing a trophy-sized fish, just remember that it took a long time and a lot of food to get him to that size. And if you don't want to have the fish mounted and hang it on your den wall, consider releasing him so someone else can enjoy the same pleasure of trying to catch him. By the time a fish surmounts all the obstacles to get that big, he's worth sharing with other anglers.

10

Ecology

Late in the 1960s when people suddenly became aroused about the shocking conditions of their environment and the devastating effects of pollution and landrape, they needed a word that would serve as a rallying cry to focus attention on the problems. Thus "ecology" was deftly liberated from the syntax of science and mustered into everyday use. Conservationists, journalists, politicians, and even housewives took up the cause of ecology, which most interpreted to mean a clean earth, free of the pollution wrought by machines of progress.

But ecology does not really mean a clean earth. Its origins reach back to the 1800s when a word was needed in the scientific community to define the study of how animals interact with their environment. Ecology, like biology or geology, is a field of study. It is the study of the way in which all the forms of life relate to their environment. The basic tenet of ecology is that life does not exist apart from its environment and that each species is, in fact, a product of its own particular environment or "ecosystem", owing its existence to factors of climate, geography, and geology.

Ecology is the dynamic aspect of nature's system. From a standpoint of fishing, it relates each fish to such factors as water conditions, nearby objects, available food, potential enemies, and even the fisherman.

A WATER ENVIRONMENT

Most animals live in an atmosphere called air, and since we humans are air-breathing animals, we are familiar with this type of environment. Fish, on the other hand, survive in a medium of water, an environment that is totally strange to us. To understand how and why a fish functions, we must first investigate its habitat. Like air, pure water is colorless, odorless, and tasteless. But water is a very heavy medium compared to air—780 times as dense—and it is extremely difficult for a fish to move through it with any ease. This density becomes apparent to us when we swim on the surface and pull our arms through the water. It is even more apparent when we dive beneath the surface and try to propel ourselves underwater. Although the denseness of the water also impedes the movement of fish to some degree, it provides a compensation of extreme value by counteracting gravity. Fish are virtually weightless creatures in the water, floating free of gravitational effects. In fact, it is precisely this neutral buoyancy that permits a fisherman to use light tackle and to lift a fish to the surface using lines with breaking strengths far below the actual weight of the fish in air.

To counteract the density of water, fish have evolved very characteristic streamlined or fusiform shapes. The fastest fish have the theoretically perfect hydrodynamic shape: blunter at the head with the greatest girth one-third of the way back tapering to a thin tail. Every part of the fish—fins, eyes, gills, body cavity—are all patterned to minimize drag through the

The two atmospheres—air and water. Living in an atmosphere of water, fish have evolved differently from mammals. To understand the way a fish functions, one must understand the water environment. ▶

water just as a jet plane is streamlined to penetrate air at high rates of speed. When you consider the relative ease and the speed with which a fish can move through water, you begin to get an idea of the power its body can generate—1/500 of a horsepower per pound of body weight. If a fish lived in air, the same amount of force would be 780 times greater.

There are many instances of anglers landing "green" fish which flop around the deck of a boat and smash everything they brush against. A single blow from the tail of a tarpon will shatter the bones in a man's leg. Regardless of size, fish are powerful creatures. They have to be to move through water.

If swimming is difficult for fish, respiration is even more difficult and poses a special problem. The air we breathe is 18 percent oxygen, but fish must breathe in water, gleaning from it the tiny amounts of dissolved oxygen it contains. Average water contains only .0006 percent oxygen, or six parts of dissolved oxygen per million parts of water. On that basis, you can readily see how critical a loss of even one part per million of dissolved oxygen can be to a fish, and two or three parts can be fatal. Therefore, fish have evolved highly complex and efficient sets of gills to strain this tiny bit of oxygen from the water and assimilate it into their blood streams.

Fish are plagued by other problems. Like humans, a fish's body is composed largely of saline water, but humans live in air and the loss or gain of water content is minimized. Not so with a fish. A fish lives in water, and only a thin layer of skin separates the saline water in the fish's body from the water on the outside. In the ocean, fish lose their vital body water continuously by osmosis through the skin and have to keep drinking sea water to replace the losses. Freshwater species have an opposite problem. In lakes and streams osmosis works in the reverse, and freshwater fish are constantly flooded by water coming in through the skin. To counter this, they must have high-powered kidneys to excrete the quantities of excess water. This also means that any dissolved matter in the water easily enters the body.

Water is a uniquely powerful solvent. It dissolves and carries numerous substances in solution upon which aquatic life depends for its existence. Dissolved oxygen, carbon dioxide, nitrogen, phosphorus, potassium, iron, and other chemicals are all found in water. And water rapidly carries away solid, liquid, and gaseous wastes. Fish can be affected by all of these and depend on many for their survival.

BODY TEMPERATURE

Fish are cold blooded and their body temperatures must fluctuate up or down depending on the temperature of the water. This puts a strain on certain physiological processes. Most fish cannot tolerate rapid warming or cooling of the surrounding water. Fortunately, water has high heat capacity; its temperature does not change as rapidly as air. Shallow water, however, is affected more quickly by changes in air temperature and fish that frequent the shallows must move off into deep water if the temperature starts to change radically. Fish kills can result from severe temperature changes.

Biologists consider temperature to be the single most important factor governing the occurrence and behavior of fish. Research on fish demonstrates that heat accelerates the life processes. For example, oxygen use of trout is four times as high in warm water as it is in cold water. To survive, fish may need twice as much oxygen in water of 65 degrees F. as they would if the water were 40 degrees F. Carp digest their food four times as fast at 79 degrees than at 50 degrees. Brook trout are not able to swim well in water over 60 degrees, and by the time it reaches 70 degrees, they are swimming so poorly that they can't catch minnows.

FOOD CHAIN

The term food chain is given to the whole ecological system that ultimately provides the food for predatory fish. In its basic form, there are four links in this food chain. First are the "producers," made up of all plant life. Plants are either found growing in the bottom or they occur as myriad floating microscopic cells known as phytoplankton. Plankton means all of the small life in the water. Phytoplankton is the plant portion and zooplankton is the animal part.

Animals that feed directly on plant life are known as the "consumers" and they include worms, shrimp, clams, insects, some fishes, and zooplankton. These form the second link in the food chain. The third link includes animals that eat the consumers, the "foragers," such as crayfish, sunfish, shiners, crappie, mackerel, and herring. And the final link in the food chain is composed of the predators—those fish that feed on the foragers. Among the predators we find the muskellunge, pike, bluefish, and tuna.

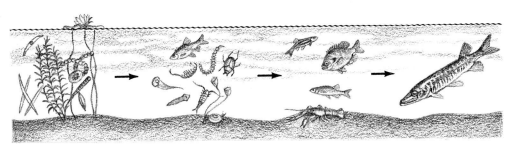

Algae and Plants   Consumers   Foragers   Predators

The food chain in its most basic form. This is the ecological system that ultimately provides food for predatory fish.

Actually, the food-chain system is not as simple as these four neat categories would imply. Many species short-circuit the food chain. For example, species like carp are both consumers and foragers. Predators like bass and trout sometimes feed on consumers as well as foragers. Some foragers like the spotted seatrout become predators at times. And so it goes. Because of these short-circuits, some ecologists prefer to call the system a food web instead of a food chain.

The food web or chain starts with the sun supplying energy to plants for photosynthesis—the process whereby light energy is used to make plant substance. The plants build their bodies from carbon, which they get from carbon dioxide gas, and other nutrients which are dissolved in the water. The abundance of plant life in any given body of water is limited by the amount of dissolved nutrients in the water, by the amount of sunlight that penetrates the water, by temperature, and by a host of other factors. With a limited amount of plant life in a body of water there will be a limited number of consumers, foragers, and predatory animals. The rule of thumb is that there is a 10 to 1 reduction of volume through each link in the food chain.

The lesson becomes apparent when we consider that to produce one 10-pound northern pike, it would take 100 pounds of minnows that ate 1,000 pounds of invertebrates that ate 10,000 pounds of plants. But let's look at it another way.

The aquatic ecosystem is a most delicate balance, and anything that affects any link in the chain will automatically affect the build up from producers, consumers, and foragers. There are some ecologists who refer to the system as a food pyramid rather than a chain or web. It is precisely this pyramid effect that severely limits the abundance of predators or gamefish. In a simplified example, there can only be one 20-pound muskie in a lake for every 100 2-pound walleyes available as prey. And it takes 32,000 1-ounce minnows (one ton) to produce the 100 walleyes that produced the one muskie and so forth. The muskie can be considered a super predator because it feeds on other predators at times and therefore is working at the top of a fifth level on the pyramid.

Predators like the pike are at the top of a pyramid, competition between various species of fish for the available forage. Some compete for bottom food, some for plankton, and others for baitfish, insects, amphibians, and other forms. The yellow perch is an example of a species that is caught in the middle. Perch live near the bottom of lakes at medium depths where they must compete with such fish as cisco and whitefish when those species are feeding on the bottom. If the perch moves toward the surface to feed on zooplankton, competition develops with the white bass, crappie, and bluegill. At the same time, the yellow perch are preyed upon by walleyes, muskellunge, pike, and often by lake trout. In the intense underwater world, perch sometimes turn the tables by feeding heavily on the fry of pike.

With the operating reduction of 10 to 1 still applying, the five-stage pyramid with the muskie at the top would require 100 *tons* of plants to produce the 10 tons of insects and worms to feed the 1 ton of minnows to get the 200 pounds of walleyes to feed the one muskie—100 tons of algae to produce one 20-pound muskie. This is a theoretical example, but a reasonable one. And it does demonstrate why the top game-fish are few and far between.

One might wonder what happened to the 100 tons of plants in our example, because all but the 20 pounds of muskie were lost somewhere along the way. Actually, the amazing reductions in the food pyramid from stage to stage do not represent losses to the ecological system of a healthy lake. The original materials produced by the plants are retained in some form and recycled through the system. Carbon dioxide given off in respiration is used again by plants in photosynthesis. Wastes excreted by the animals are converted by natural means back into basic nutrients (nitrogen, phosphates, and so forth) and are recycled. All dead organisms are reconverted by bacteria back into the basic nutrients to be used by the plants (the producers) to photosynthesize and recycle them through the food chain. In this way, the bacteria have often been referred to as a fifth link in the food chain—"the decomposers."

CARRYING CAPACITY

Quite logically, the main concern of those who study the ecology of fishes is the condition of the water. Water quality and condition not only affect fish directly, but also affects the whole aquatic chain of life leading up to the food fish eat. By knowing certain characteristics of a lake, the ecologist can determine how many fish it can support of various sizes of any particular species or all species combined. There is a very definite ceiling or carrying capacity that limits the pounds of fish (or "biomass" as it is known in ecological terminology) any body of water can support in a given period. This carrying capacity is controlled by ecological base conditions of the lake. The ecological base conditions govern the lake's "biological productivity," or primary food supply, ranging from tiny one-celled algae to planktonic invertebrates to baitfish.

One limitation on the number of fish that can be crowded into a single lake or pond is the reaction of fish to each other. Experiments have shown that many species of fish react adversely to overcrowding just as people do. If, for example, there are more of a species in a certain lake than the carrying capacity will permit, certain fish—goldfish, carp, bigmouth buffalo—excrete chemicals into the water which prevent the females from laying their eggs. Some biologists believe this may be true of largemouth bass because the most abundant spawning stocks often breed poorly and produce the fewest fry. When populations are high, one doctrine espouses, fewer young will be produced and when populations are low, more young will be produced. This seems to apply to fish as well as land animals.

OXYGEN LIMITATIONS

Oxygen is a most critical ecological limitation. As we pointed out earlier, fish must have abundant dissolved oxygen in the waters around them. Let's take it a step further. The oxygen gets into water from either the plant life below or the air above. In sunshine, aquatic plants take in carbon dioxide from the water and release pure oxygen. Clean, clear water with a healthy growth of rooted plants or floating algae is usually well-oxygenated and productive of fish life. The air acts as a buffer, supplying additional oxygen through the surface if the water is depleted below the saturation level, while oxygen will pass from the water to the air if the water is oversaturated. Thus the water and air will reach a balance at a point where the water is fully saturated. However, this

Aquatic plants supply much of the oxygen that supports fish life. Additional oxygen passes into the water from the air, when the supply gets low, but this is a slow process and a lake will die without adequate oxygen from aquatic vegetation.

exchange is slow, and lakes and estuarine waters may run out of oxygen in the course of heavy summer die-offs of aquatic growth, because the bacteria necessary for decomposition use up the oxygen supply.

Murky, overfertilized, polluted water is usually oxygen poor and unproductive. When the dissolved oxygen is diminished below the normal amount by 20 or 30 percent, fish have trouble with feeding, growth, self-protection, and other vital activities. If oxygen is lowered by 50 percent or more, the fish die from suffocation.

Oxygen problems often arise in the winter when our northern lakes freeze over. The ice, of course, prevents the air from coming in contact with the surface of the water and there is no exchange of oxygen that way. Under ordinary circumstances, however, the plants usually get enough sunlight through clear ice to produce the oxygen needed by fish. But when there is snow cover, the light is blocked out and plants can no longer photosynthesize. Oxygen levels can fall from completely saturated to almost totally depleted in two or three days, and the fish can perish from lack of oxygen in what is known as a winter fishkill. Seven and one-half inches of clear ice only blocks out about 15 percent of the light reaching the plants, but 5 inches of dry snow on top of the ice can block out 97 percent of the light. As a rule of thumb, the amount of light that penetrates 1 to 2 feet of fairly clear ice is sufficient for photosynthesis.

TURBIDITY

Silt is another extremely detrimental factor in aquatic habitats. Because silt affects the clarity of the water, it screens out sunlight, preventing photosynthesis and subsequent oxygen formation. Equally significant is the tendency of silt to settle on the bottom. As the silt settles, it covers the bottom with unhealthy ooze that smothers plants and destroys or buries delicate aquatic creatures including the eggs of some fish. In Oklahoma, biologists demonstrated that clear ponds were 13 times as productive of basic foods for fish than dirty ones. Researchers have found that silt interferes with the activities of fish. Heavy silt action, for example, caused largemouth bass to slow down their rate of swimming. Both bass and green sunfish coughed repeatedly when they were placed in highly turbid water, apparently in an effort to clean their gills of silt.

Fish bite poorly in turbid waters according to Illinois biologist G. W. Bennett, who measures water transparency by how far a small white disk (Secchi disk) is visible through the water. In his book *Management of Lakes and Ponds*, Bennett states, "In most small lakes and ponds, fishing is poor if the transparency of the water is less than 2 feet (Secchi disk). Fly casting is probably best when the transparency of the water ranges between 3.5 and 6.0 feet. When the transparency becomes greater than 6.0 feet, fish are able to see the angler for some distance and unless long casts are made to place the angler beyond the fish's vision, or extreme care is taken to shield his movements from the fish, the rate of catch will decrease as the water becomes clearer."

LAKE SIZE AND PRODUCTIVITY

Scientists have learned that the physical shape and size of lakes, reservoirs, and estuaries influence their productivity. A medium-size lake appears to yield the highest productivity in pounds of fish per acre of water surface. Other things being equal, between 1,000 and 5,000 acres is about the optimum size for a lake. The trouble is that in ecology "other things" are seldom equal. Factors tend to vary extensively and the whole issue becomes confused. For example, whatever its size, a shallow lake is more productive acre by acre than a deeper one simply because sunlight can penetrate to the bottom more readily. And that clarity enhances productivity because clear, silt-free water allows maximum sunlight penetration.

For similar reasons, narrow streams are more productive acre by acre than wide streams, particularly if they are clear. Paul Needham in his book *Trout Streams* reported that bottoms of streams averaging 3 feet wide produced three times more invertebrate food for fish per acre than streams that averaged 40 feet wide. Needham's data was compiled on New York State streams and his studies show that the greatest difference in productivity is between streams that are more or less than 10 feet wide, as shown in the following table.

Stream Width (In Feet)	Amount of Food on Bottom (Pounds Per Acre)
1-6	197
7-12	160
13-18	90
19-50	57

In the United States, southern lakes are considered to be more productive than northern ones because of the longer growing season. Therefore much higher yields should be available from fish populations in southern states. In Louisiana, for example, lakes should yield 118 percent of their carrying capacity at any particular instant through the year, according to Bennett. But in Tennessee, the yield should be 86 percent, in Illinois 50 percent, and in Wisconsin only 39 percent of the carrying capacity.

STRATIFICATION OF LAKES

To understand how temperature of the water affects fish, we must first focus on the series of changes a lake or pond undergoes during the year. From limnology (study of lakes) we know that these changes are predictable, strongly dictating what you can expect to catch and how you must fish. As water becomes colder it gets denser, or heavier. The heavier water will sink toward the bottom of a lake and remain there. Water is heaviest at 39.2 degrees Fahrenheit, but water colder than this becomes increasingly less dense, or lighter, down to 32 degrees F. When water freezes it is less dense than the surrounding water, and the ice will float on the surface. Otherwise, ice would sink to the bottom of northern lakes in the winter and by accumulating would kill all life in them.

But because the ice floats and forms on the surface, the top of the lake can freeze solid and insulate the rest of the lake against freezing. The cold air stays above the ice and the water below the ice is warmer than 32 degrees F. In fact, once a coating of ice shields the surface from wind, there are very few currents in a lake to disturb the tranquility until the following spring. When the ice melts, the sun warms the surface waters, while winds help to mix the surface water and shift it downward. At the same time, as the water on the surface warms toward 39.2 degrees F., it becomes heavier and sinks to the bottom. Water on the bottom is then displaced and forced toward the surface where it is re-oxygenated. As this takes place, the lake is said to "overturn," and a

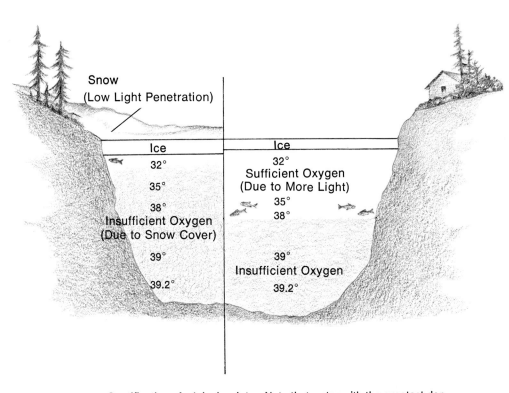

Snow
(Low Light Penetration)

Ice

Ice

32°

32°
Sufficient Oxygen
(Due to More Light)

35°

35°

38°

38°

Insufficient Oxygen
(Due to Snow Cover)

39°

39°
Insufficient Oxygen

39.2°

39.2°

Stratification of a lake in winter. Note that water with the greatest density (39.2°F.) sinks to the bottom while the lighter water (32°F.) stays
on top. Part of the lake covered by snow and ice *(left)* has low light
penetration, hence insufficient oxygen to support fish life except near
the top. Sufficient oxygen can penetrate part of lake covered by ice
only *(right)*, providing a larger area in which fish can live.

brief balance is reached when all of the water is about the
same temperature.

When the temperature is uniform for that short period, fish
may be found at any level. But as the sun continues to warm
the surface temperatures, many lakes become stratified.
Three distinct layers form in the lake based on water temperature. The warm surface layer is called the *epilimnion*, while
the cold bottom layer of water is known as the *hypolimnion*.
In between, there is a small transitional zone of rapid temperature change called the *thermocline*. By definition the thermocline is a layer where temperature changes at least one-
half a degree per foot of depth.

There are a number of factors that determine how deep each of these layers will be, how fast they form, and the amount of temperature differential. The depth of the lake and its shape play a part. So do prevailing winds, elevation, location, and even the color of the water. Turbid water is darker and therefore will absorb heat faster than lighter water, which tends to reflect the heat.

During summer, the epilimnion or upper warm area increases in depth as the temperatures continue to warm the waters. And the epilimnion is usually thicker in large lakes than in smaller ones. In the typical warmwater lake or reser-

Stratification of a lake in summer. The water has separated into layers according to temperature. Comfort zones for various species of game-fish are also shown. Note that most fish prefer the area of the thermocline where temperature is between 60° and 75°.

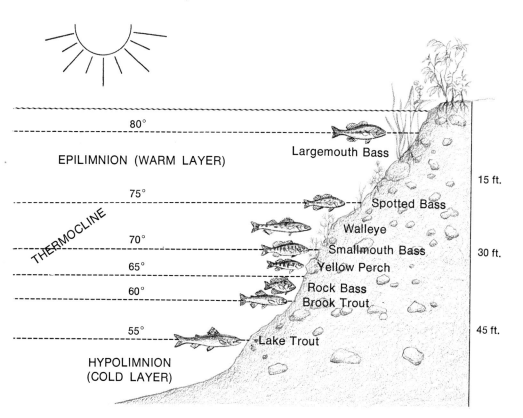

voir, the hypolimnion, or cold lower region, loses its oxygen
as the summer progresses, because there is no photosynthesis
there to produce oxygen and there is a great deal of bacterial
decomposition of the dead organic material that sinks down
from the upper layers. Decomposition, as we said, uses
oxygen. Naturally, there can be no fish life at all in a lower
coldwater layer totally devoid of oxygen. If because of this
factor, the total water area of a lake cannot be utilized, the
lake, from a fish's standpoint, is much shallower than it
appears to us.

In the fall, as the sun moves farther south and the air temperatures cool, the surface waters of the warmwater lake also
begin to cool down. The cooling surface water becomes heavier and will start to sink toward the bottom, forcing the now
lighter lower water toward the surface. Another "overturn" of
the lake is created and the point is reached where the temperatures throughout the lake are uniform once more. Then the
surface waters continue to drop in temperature and ice eventually forms, thus completing the cycle.

TEMPERATURE PREFERENCES IN LAKES

It is worth repeating that water temperature is the single
most important factor in determining where fish will be,
assuming, of course, that there will be an adequate supply of
dissolved oxygen at the depth where the preferred temperature occurs. No matter where you fish, you should know the
water temperature at different depths and make certain that
it is within the comfort range of the species you seek.

The table on facing page includes the preferred temperatures for some species as they appear in scientific records.
Some are based on limited observations in specific lakes, while
others are more general. Although they cannot be considered
applicable to all waters, they do offer an idea of the differences
one will encounter among the various species of gamefish.

These temperature ranges apply to the average member of
the species. Fish can and do exist at higher and lower temperatures. Yet, as a starting point, it makes sense to fish to stay in

Species	Range of Preferred Temperatures
Atlantic salmon	57-61
Pacific salmon	53-55
Coho salmon	52-57
Brook trout	53-65
Yellow perch	60-70
Striped bass	56-61
Largemouth bass	68-75
Smallmouth bass	65-71
Spotted bass	74-76
Walleye	60-70
Rock bass	59-70
Muskellunge	60-70
Northern pike	50-70
Panfish	65-75
Lake trout	45-55

those zones where the temperatures are well within the comfort range of the fish.

One of the most useful tools that a fisherman can carry with him is a thermometer. There are many types available on the market, but the most useful ones are electronic thermometers that are lowered on a wire. The wire is marked in some manner so you can determine depth, and the thermometer will read the temperature at any depth within a few seconds. Temperatures appear on a calibrated micro-volt-meter.

If you want to measure subsurface temperatures less expensively, you can do it by rigging a container that will bring up water quickly from a specified depth. These containers usually have a cork that can be pulled out after they are lowered to the required depth. It is important to operate so that the water sample from the depth you want is not mixed with the water above. You can then measure the temperature of your sample with a regular mercury thermometer which should register within a few tenths of a degree of the temperature below. However, it should be pointed out that this method can be slow when you're trying to locate a thermocline or a specific temperature. With the electronic models, you can continue to lower them slowly and take readings along the way.

STRATIFICATION IN SALT WATER

The ocean and some deeper bays are layered just like lakes, and fish spend most of their time in the zone that suits their temperature preferences. For example, bluefish can tolerate water from 52 to 80 degrees, but they often prefer a temperature around 67 degrees. Consequently, they may remain at a reasonable depth below the warmer surface waters at the top of the thermocline, which may be 25 to 35 feet deep. But for feeding, they will often rise into surface waters where the temperature may be 70 degrees or higher.

In the fall of the year when the thermocline is erased, bluefish might be found at any level and often near the bottom because the temperature at this time should be about the same at any layer. In fact, it's generally around 56 degrees along the mid-Atlantic coast. By this time, the water temperature is below their normal preference, but they may remain in the area if the bait supply is heavy as long as the temperature does not drop below their minimum tolerance level. More than likely, the bluefish will start moving offshore and to the south when temperatures fall, feeding on the bottom along the way, and traveling until they find more comfortable water for their winter residence.

As an interesting sidelight, biologists have learned that during the summer along the northeast Atlantic coast, certain winds can drive cold water shoreward, and when this happens, bluefishing falls off. The bluefish will move out of the area rapidly and won't return until the shift in the winds brings warmer water.

Marine fishery biologists have found that oceanic big-game fish live in restricted temperature ranges just as freshwater fish do. White-marlin anglers know that unless they can find water temperatures of 68 degrees (and preferably 70 degrees) or higher along the 20-fathom curve, their chances of taking whites are almost nonexistent. Tuna, swordfish, dolphin, and almost any other pelagic species are temperature oriented.

Shallow flats warm much faster than deeper water, but they also cool off very quickly. The permit will seldom be found on a flat when the water temperature is less than 70 degrees. Snook are particularly sensitive to temperature and so are bonefish. We were in the Florida Keys not long ago and witnessed a period when low water temperatures on the flats delayed the annual spring invasion of migratory tarpon for a full two weeks. A cold front had chilled the shallow waters and constant winds prevented them from reheating.

Atlantic mackerel concentrate in temperatures of 48 to 52 degrees in their spring migration northward. Striped bass also migrate northward along the Atlantic coast in the spring, pushing on as the limiting water-temperature boundary of 48 to 52 degrees gradually moves northeasterly. Along parts of the coast, there is an exceptionally cold wall of water that prevents the migratory striped bass from entering the area until later in the spring. Yet local stocks of the fish can be found in bays and estuaries where they may have wintered. The local fish come out of hibernation and start active feeding as temperatures rise into the upper 40s.

WATER MOVEMENT

The way in which water moves plays an important role in the ecology of fishing. Tides, currents, river flows, and the water level in lakes and impoundments all affect the habits and occurrence of fishes.

Moving water provides gamefish with two distinct advantages: it carries food to them, and it disorients their prey, making it easier for them to feed. Since it would be exhausting for any fish to remain in rapidly moving water for long periods of time, most fish are found along the edges of a moving current or fast water, or behind an obstruction that breaks the force of the water flow. With its powerful tail, the feeding predator can propel itself rapidly into the current, strike its prey, and then work toward quieter water as the current carries it downstream. With simple fin steering, the fish can reach the edge of the fast current and swim easily back to its lie in more placid water. Gamefish are masters of turbulence, shore current, river flow, back eddy, tailrace tiderip, and other situations that improve the chances for an easy meal.

The best strategy in fishing a current is to cast upcurrent or upstream in such a way that your offering follows the natural path of the water. Fish are looking for their meals coming from that direction and they will probably see and react to your offering.

TIDES

To the saltwater angler, tides are not only important but may be critical. Many inshore areas only contain fish on a certain stage of the tide and then only for an hour or two. The rest of the time, the entire area may be void of fish. Fish, of course, always face into a tide or current, and if you're fishing from a bridge, the better side is the uptide side of the structure. In fact, the fish often lie behind the pilings to break the current while they watch for food being swept by.

Generally speaking, if you find fish at a particular location on a certain stage of the tide, and weather or temperature doesn't fluctuate much, you'll probably find fish there again the next day only the time will be one hour later—the time of the next day's tide. Tides are caused mainly by the gravitational effect of the moon and to a lesser degree by the sun. The sun is really insignificant in its relationship to tides and for practical purposes, it can be ignored. On the new and full moons, the tides are somewhat higher and lower than they are during other times of the month. In many areas, you'll find that fishing is better during those periods because the fish can sometimes invade areas that they cannot reach under normal tidal conditions. Not only are the times of the tides important, but the tidal range or the amount of rise or fall can be equally important. Fishermen look for the widest range in the tides. Top anglers are keen students of fish behavior. Fishing guides in the Florida Keys, for example, often amaze their clients by staking out in a particular location and announcing that the fish will be along within a half hour. What they have done is staked out along a route normally taken by fish on a particular stage of the tide and they know by experience and observation that when conditions reach a certain level, the fish will be along. We have observed in South and Central America that fishing along the shoreline of the Pacific falls off sharply on the last half of the falling tide and the first part of the incoming. It's best when the water is a couple of hours before flood and for the first two hours afterward. As a general rule, if an estuarine system of bays and marshes is drained through a few narrow openings to the sea, you can always expect to find gamefish waiting at the narrow inlet or channels when the outgoing tide reaches a good velocity, sweeping food from the shallow bays seaward.

11

Conservation

Conservation can be defined as the protection of our environment and the enforcement of ecological health. It has become one of the great popular movements of the century, bringing together millions of people in a common cause a-gainst pollution and other environmental assaults.

Fishermen have been leaders in the conservation battle for a long time, longer than most newcomers to the scene realize. It has been a tough and frustrating battle up to now and it's going to become more difficult before it is over. Any angler who is unwilling to stay informed on conservation matters and fails to lend his support should be prepared to give up his hobby entirely. The day may well come when there are not many places left to fish.

OUR WATER SUPPLY

In the United States elaborate programs of water management are essential, not only to quench our national thirst but to control floods, to provide water for boat traffic, to benefit wildlife, and to have a clean water in which to fish. We appear to be approaching a time when all the fresh water in our country will be under some sort of control. Rivers, diversion channels, reservoirs, dams, canals, and aqueducts will be integrated into great interlocking systems so that every drop of fresh water can be measured, treated, and scheduled for use. So far, we have tried to solve our problems mainly by diverting water from areas of plenty to areas of scarcity via pipes, aqueducts, and diversion channels, and by storing water behind dams in order to provide a supply in the dry season. Now we are gradually beginning to realize that pollution control has been the missing ingredient.

The total yearly use of water in the United States, 124 million million gallons, is only 1/150 of the 20 million *billion* gallons supplied annually by precipitation (at a national average of 30 inches of precipitation per square inch). Thus it would seem that we have more than an ample supply. But we lose 60 percent to evaporation, and we must manage on the 40 percent of rain and snow that eventually flows on to the sea. This would still appear to allow a great surplus—60 times our need—with proper distribution facilities. Yet, in the United States, water famine has troubled farmers for decades and recently has threatened many urban centers, including Los Angeles, Miami, and New York.

Many of the urban centers have good watersheds but face shortages because they are polluting the very rivers and lakes that could otherwise furnish the clean water they need. Industrial and municipal pollution has so damaged New York's Hudson River, for example, that it cannot be used for the city's water supply. The Hudson carries an average of 8 billion gallons of fresh water past New York City and out to sea *every day of the year*. This is enough water to provide 40 million people with 200 gallons per day each if it could be fully utilized. Yet, the river is too polluted to use and New York City has been unable at times to provide a daily supply of 150 gallons for each of its 10 million people.

SEWAGE AND EUTROPHICATION

Sewage contamination is the foremost water-pollution problem in most communities today. Raw sewage contains pathogenic bacteria that can cause human diseases such as typhoid and hepatitis. These and various gastro-enteric diseases may be contracted from eating raw shellfish that live in sewage-polluted waters. Health authorities have closed more than a million acres of the best shellfish beds in United States waters because of pollution. Segments of the shellfish industry have been abruptly and totally put out of business, with economic losses running to tens of millions of dollars per year. And no one need tell you that sewage-polluted waters are unfit for swimming and water skiing.

In spite of the fact that more and more communities are constructing central treatment systems to render sewage as harmless to human health as possible, there are still a great number of communities that follow the practice of dumping raw sewage into the nearest available waterway. But even the treatment plants fall short of solving the problem of ecologic health of our waters. Most treatments do not remove enough of the nutrient materials that cause overfertilization of aquatic plant life—phosphorus, nitrogen, and others. They merely dissolve them into the effluent water. When the dissolved nutrients enter lakes or estuaries, they trigger a series of unfortunate events called "eutrophication" (over-fertilization) described in the following passage by A. Hassler and B. Ingersoll.

> First, the algae population skyrockets in a man-fertilized lake. Water fleas (miniature freshwater shrimp), the staple diet of fry and minnows, cannot eat enough algae to keep these plants in check. As a result, billions of algae live their languid lives, reproduce, and then die. As they drift toward the bottom, their decomposing bodies exhaust the deepwater oxygen supply. Trout, whitefish, and other species suffocate in the oxygen-thin depths.
>
> The lake's ecology, initially upset by excess nutrients, then becomes totally upended, since bacteria can convert only

some of the dead algae into plant and animal food. Therefore, generation after generation of algae settle on the bottom,
adding layer after layer to the muck. The rate of sedimentation
is most rapid in a northern lake where bacteria grow only
during the summer while nutrients are added throughout the
year. As erosion and sedimentation fill in the lake, shoreline
vegetation impinges on the open water. In time, the lake
becomes shallow and overgrown. So much so, that it becomes
a marsh or a bog. The accelerated process of aging has taken
its toll: the lake's life is ended.

Hassler and Ingersoll report that more than one-third of
the 100,000 lakes in the United States are showing signs of
reaching this alarming condition of eutrophication.

If you've been wondering why some communities have
been banning the use of detergents, consider that over 75
percent of the phosphates in sewage effluents originate from
household detergents. The fertilizers used on our farms and
the ones we put in our backyards also add greatly to the
problem as they are washed by rain into the waterways. The
much lamented Lake Erie, for example, is being shepherded
to its impending death by the phosphates and nitrates found
in sewage and fertilizers. That doesn't mean that pesticides
and industrial wastes don't take their toll and add to the
demise, but the tendency in the past has been to overlook the
damage done by eutrophication. Each year, Lake Erie is
forced to swallow up some 70 million pounds of nitrogen
from commercial fertilizers, while municipal sewage
contributes a generous 90 million pounds. You can readily see
that the effects of fertilizers are nearly as great as sewage.

Of course, some nitrates and phosphates are needed for
normal, healthy growth, but the right quantity is far less than
we now have in our polluted waters.

BACTERIA

Many types of bacteria thrive well in polluted waters.
Scientist Barry Commoner reported that the total bacteria
content of the waters of New York Harbor increased by *ten
to twenty times* in the short span of only twenty years—from

the mid-1940s to the mid-1960s. Health officials are fully aware of this fact, but they can't really explain it. They thought they were doing enough in adding sewage facilities to at least hold the line, but obviously further efforts are needed.

Federal biologists David Deuel and J. Mahoney recorded an incredible series of disease epidemics among the fish in New York's harbor waters in the late 1960s that were traced to pollution. As many as seventeen species of fish were attacked in a single year by an often fatal bacterial disease known as finrot which erodes away the skin, fins and tail. In 1968, these two biologists found that 80 percent of the bluefish in the area came down with finrot. The bacteria that attacked these fish were marine types obviously cultured into high abundance by the sewage in the harbor waters.

Estuarine lagoons and many lakes are polluted seriously by cesspools or septic tanks. As the pools and tanks drain into the ground, their leachings flow into the waterways, supplying heavy loads of dissolved nutrients to overfertilize plant life and cause eutrophication. Biologists Hassler and Ingersoll noted that it took the seepage from only seven cottages to change Cochran Lake, ". . .once a pure gem set in the northern Wisconsin wilds into a 300-acre caldron of pea soup."

SEDIMENTATION

Silt washed off the land into the water causes unhealthy conditions for fish. Experiments with pike show that a deposition rate of 1/25 of an inch of silt per day was enough to kill 97 percent of pike eggs in South Dakota lakes. M. Trautman concluded that the principal reason for the decline of the pike, walleyes, catfish, buffalo, suckers, and drum in Ohio waters is siltation. Here's the way Trautman put it: "Clayey soils, suspended in water, prohibited the proper penetration of light; thereby preventing development of the aquatic vegetation, of the food of fishes, of fish eggs, and fry. Settling over the formerly clean bottoms, silt destroyed the habitat of those fish species requiring bottoms of sand, gravel, boulders, bedrock, or organic debris."

The combination of silt and organic fallout that builds up on the bottom becomes a repository for all sorts of foul substances, DDT, oil (which clings to silt particles and sinks), lead, mercury, and anaerobic bacteria. Unfortunately this silt does not remain in place on the bottom. Boat traffic, wind and currents stir up the silt to contaminate the water above. Through eutrophication, the process of decay and sedimentation, lakes and estuaries hasten to their death. An obvious, but difficult solution to the siltation problem is to correct soil erosion throughout the watershed. Reduction of organic pollution would reduce sedimentation from decaying organisms.

As California stream biologists Cordone and Kelly put it, "*First*, there has been sufficient work done to establish the fact that sediment is harmful to trout and salmon streams. *Second*, our experience in the Sierra Nevada indicates that the bulk of damage there is totally unnecessary. It can be prevented with known land use methods."

STRIP MINING

Whereas Trautman found siltation the worst type of pollution in Ohio lakes, Frank Graham, in his book *Disaster by Default*, found strip mines to be the worst offenders in the coal mining states of Appalachia—Pennsylvania, Ohio, Kentucky, and West Virginia. He quoted Pennsylvania's Senator Joseph Clark as listing strip mining as "the toughest resource problem in America today." Senator Clark warned that no single approach seemed to solve this problem. It has sterilized thousands of miles of streams—2,000 miles in Pennsylvania alone—strangled the economic life of hundreds of communities, killed billions of fish, and rendered the prospects of many areas of the region dim. The alternative, according to Senator Clark, is a massive assault on strip mining to bring it under control. Strip miners leave huge, ugly scars across the face of the earth that leach sulphuric acid into the nearest waterways. This acid mine drainage pollutes streams and lakes, raising the acidity of the water above the tolerable level. As the acid precipitates out, it coats the stream beds with orange-colored residue to remind everyone of its presence.

Acids disrupt the ecology of streams and either damage or kill fish by depressing their respiration and causing acute irritation to gills and other sensitive membranes. How serious is the problem? The Federal Water Pollution Control Administration recently reported 61,000 fish killed in one year by one strip mine, and even though it is a federal crime to mine in this way, the Administrative agency noted that this same mine kills fish every year. But strip mines are only part of the industrial pollution scene.

INDUSTRIAL POLLUTION

A great variety of toxic substances are disposed of in public waters by manufacturing industries. Factories are located on waterways for the major purpose of simplifying their disposal problems. And those waterways inherit all types of toxic effluents from manufacturing processes, regardless of whether the end products are chemicals, cloth, synthetic fibers, fertilizers, or any of hundreds of other items. Plating mills dispose of cyanide and other pollutants. Paper and pulp mills give off sulphide wastes, lignin, and other by-products that deplete oxygen levels.

Metals in solution at very low levels are lethal to fish. Lead is deadly at 0.3 parts per million of water (ppm), copper at 0.5 ppm, and zinc at 0.5 ppm. In even such small amounts, metals damage the gills and mucous membranes causing fish to suffocate. Nickel, mercury, cadmium, and cobalt all have the same effect. Cyanides (lethal at more than 0.05 ppm) and sulphides are acids and they will kill or damage fish. Ammonia and chlorine cause congestion of membranes and nervous spasms. Fluorine, with prolonged exposure at 5 ppm or more, causes death through nervous disorder.

A shocking example of industrial pollution is the 1963 disaster in the Roanoke River, as taken from a report of the Sport Fishing Institute of Washington, D.C.

An extensive kill of sea-run striped bass (rockfish) spawning stocks, channel catfish, and a variety of other species occurred in the Roanoke River, from Weldon, North Carolina, 115 miles downstream below Jamesville, during a one week period in April 1963. Sport fishermen first observed rockfish in trouble at three a.m., Sunday morning, April 21, at the height of the rockfishing season. The kill totaled 18,000 to 22,000 fish, weighing between 37 and 45 tons. Average weight was a bit under four pounds, with many females, some weighing up to 35 pounds, apparently killed in the act of spawning. The source was found to be a spill of wastes from a paper mill containing resin acid soaps which occurred when the 'black liquid feed tank' spilled over for eight minutes early Sunday morning. The overflow, 10,000 to 15,000 gallons, ran down a ditch and into the river.

Each year, the federal government lists all reported fish kills, and one such report recently listed 11.6 *million* fish killed in a single year. Over 8 million of these were destroyed by industrial pollution (including food processing plants), nearly 2 million by farm wastes, and about 3/4 million by city wastes. This doesn't include the millions more that were killed during the same period and not reported to the government for inclusion in the statistics.

This federal fish kill report cites some dramatic tales of mayhem and disaster. Manure wastes from livestock feedlots got into a stream and promptly destroyed a quarter of a million fish. Dairy wastes in a stream killed another 50,000 fish. A sewage plant out of commission for a little over three hours poured wastes directly into a stream and 3,000 fish suffered the consequences. A mystery chemical spilled while pumping a barge killed between 10,000 and 100,000 fish. Cyanide from a metal treatment company passed into a sewer, reached an adjacent stream, and 4,100 fish were destroyed. Fly-ash wastes from power plants killed 163,000 and 54,000 fish respectively in two separate incidents. And these are only a few examples from comprehensive lists.

The total loss from pollution in our sample year is many times the 11.6 million fish reported to the federal government. Obvious fish kills are only part of the story. Biologists know that fish populations are held down by contamination of their habitat. Then there are situations where spawning fish are destroyed as we found in the Roanoke River. Unless a fish kill occurs in one short stretch of a waterway and in sufficient quantity, it is seldom noticed or reported. In polluted water, fish may have trouble feeding, reproducing, breathing, and resisting disease. In this way alone, fish populations can be devastated without any fish kills being reported. Even in the rare instance where a company must make reparations and pay damages, how do you measure the net worth of a fish population? How do you calculate the loss of a waterway for an indefinite period of time? How do you place a value on the eggs and fry that were lost or the disruption of spawning which will affect future generations of the species? And assuming that you could make all these calculations and enforce a judgment against a polluter, where are you going to get the fish to replace the ones that were destroyed? Ask yourself these questions and you'll find that the answer lies in stopping industrial pollution at the source.

THERMAL POLLUTION

Although pollution has dramatic aspects, it usually works slowly and insidiously to undermine the ecologic health of aquatic habitats, eroding the food chain, weakening the fish, and preventing breeding. Most types of pollution have been with us for a long time, but there is a new, large-scale threat to hundreds of lakes, streams, and estuaries in thermal pollution—hot water effluents from large plants and, more specifically, the giant thermonuclear power plants now being rushed into construction to feed our national appetite for electricity.

In a power plant, the energy of nuclear fuel is used to produce steam at high pressure. The steam turns the turbine, which powers the generator. However, once it has gone through the turbine, the spent steam must be recondensed into water, which is done by cooling it in a condenser with

Underwater photo of an area devastated by thermal pollution. The bottom grasses and macroalgae are dead or dying due to high temperature and effluent water from a nearby power plant. Water temperature in this area has exceeded 100°F.

water taken from a lake, river, estuary, bay, or ocean. Of the 60,000 billion gallons of water per year now used by American industry for cooling, about three-quarters is used in power-plant steam condensers. As of now, thermal pollution has erupted as a problem only in some limited areas. However, power development apparently is not going to wait for technology to provide easy answers to pollution problems.

To some people, it may seem strange that a temperature rise of "only" 10 or 20 degrees F. in the vicinity of a power plant could be ecologically damaging. The difficulty stems from the fact that there is a limit to how much an organism's metabolism can be wound up by rising temperature. The biochemical processes run faster and faster until the delicate mechanisms that keep all running smoothly together are overtaxed and begin to operate abnormally. Then the animal ceases to reproduce properly and suffers internal disorders that can lead to ill health or even death.

Such consequences may result from a rise of only a few degrees when temperatures are naturally high. The limits of tolerance are sharply defined for each species. Lake trout can tolerate water temperatures of up to 77 degrees F. However, satisfactory growth of their young cannot take place in waters over 68 degrees F., and spawning will not occur at temperatures above 48 degrees F.

Higher temperatures result in faster development and hatching of eggs; but beyond a certain point, the biochemistry goes awry and the eggs develop abnormally or not at all. Carp eggs exposed to temperatures between 68 and 75 degrees F. will not undergo cell division. The Oregon Fish Commission, for example, says that if the temperature of the Columbia River is increased by only 5.4 degrees F., hatchability of Chinook salmon eggs will decline disastrously.

Power companies, in business for a profit, like to keep costs down. Therefore, they prefer to discharge heat into natural waters first, cooling reservoirs second, and cooling towers third. The ecologist favors the reverse order, because whole ecosystems can be thrown out of balance by excess heat. Before long, many natural waters will reach the limit of their heat-absorbing capacity. Then, energy consumers—homeowners and industries alike—will have to pay the full cost of the product they buy instead of letting the environment pay part of the bill.

OIL POLLUTION

The dangers of oil pollution came dramatically to public attention in the late 1960s when the Torrey Canyon and Ocean Eagle disasters were quickly followed by the Santa Barbara incident. Oil clung to particles and sank or floated across the surface of the water for dozens and even hundreds of miles to destroy delicate estuarine and beach ecosystems. Scientists

on the scene in some areas of major oil spills predict that it
will take years and years before the environment recovers.

Oil pollution is not new. It has been with us for many
years, insidiously ruining some of our best fishing waters.
There are a variety of sources from which oil pollution
emanates. Most pollution that affects fish comes from
accidental spillage by tankers, from offshore towers, or from
storage facilities. The practice in the past was for tankers to
pump oil into the water while cleaning their tanks, but this
practice is being discouraged and it is hoped that it will cease
in the near future.

Slow but constant leakage and infiltration from refineries
or offshore seepage is still a major source of oil pollution in
our waterways. Unfortunately, it is a difficult situation to
remedy. Careless handling at plants also results in
by-products such as cresols and phenols getting loose. And
when petroleum is lost in production or from storage
facilities, it usually finds its way to the nearest water.

Petroleum products can be exceedingly dangerous to
aquatic life. Oil, gasoline, kerosene, and tar kill fish and reduce
oxygen exchange from air to water. Phenols, cresols, and
other petroleum by-products are toxic in small amounts—5 to
10 parts per million—causing nervous disorders, paralysis,
upset of equilibrium, and even death to fishes. There are
other damaging but non-lethal effects. For example, oysters
seem unable to breed in the vicinity of refineries. In less than
lethal amounts, petroleum products taint the flesh of fishes,
making them inedible. It is most discouraging for an angler
to come home with a 10-pound striped bass only to have it
rejected at the table by his wife and kids because it tastes like
an oily rag.

REPELLANTS

Some ninety years ago, Frank Buckland correlated the
normal behavior of gamefishes to the danger from the smells
of various pollutants. He concluded, in his *Natural History of
British Fishes*, that "the lordly salmon will not put in an

appearance where his regal nose is likely to be offended by unsavoury smells."

A modern researcher, J. B. Sprague, followed up Buckland's theory experimentally and in 1964 reported that salmon migrating downstream would avoid going into water with tiny amounts of copper pollution. At a concentration of only 2/100 of a part per million of water, salmon were repulsed even though they could stay alive in water with up to twenty times this amount of copper. No wonder so many of our man polluted bays are no longer visited by masses of migratory gamefish each summer.

PESTICIDES

Pesticides have contaminated the whole earth, but nowhere is this threat worse than in the waterways of our country. Lakes, rivers, and estuaries receive almost all contaminating substances, such as pesticides, that are washed off the land. Insecticides in harmful concentrations become paralytic nerve poisons to fishes, causing lack of coordination, erratic behavior, loss of equilibrium, muscle spasms, convulsions, and finally, cessation of respiration. The complex aquatic food chains transmit and concentrate pesticides and other dangerous substances to the point where physiological damage short of death can render animals incapable of reproduction and other vital functions. In less than lethal amounts, the poisons build up in smaller animals of the food chain on a cumulative basis until such concentrations make them poisoned bait for gamefish or other predatory animals.

From W. H. Stickel, an expert on pesticides, we learn that the sheer force of multiple applications is one cause for concern. Animals that safely store or metabolize the amount of persistent chemical received from one application may find their facilities swamped by the second, third, or thirteenth application. Under certain circumstances, for example, two applications of DDT at 0.5 lb./acre have killed fish. Most of the chlorinated hydrocarbon insecticides, including DDT, will decrease the production of plankton by 50 to 90 percent at levels of only one part per million. Isopod and amphipod crustaceans, which are important in the food chains of salt marshes, were nearly extirpated by 0.2 lb./acre of DDT in one test and failed to recover within two years.

Any amount above 1/10 part of insecticide to 1 million parts of water (0.1 PPM) of the chlorinated hydrocarbons—DDT, parathion, malathion, endrin, dieldrin, toxaphene, lindane, or heptachlor—may be lethal to fish and aquatic life. The worst is DDT which is known to keep its potency for at least fifteen years and probably much longer than that. And the final outcome is usually death by suffocation.

A classic case was recorded a few years back when two biologists, Drs. Harrington and Bidlingmeyer, heard that a tidal marsh near Florida's Indian River was to be bombed with an insecticide called dieldrin. They arranged to be on hand to study the effects and reported the following:

> Two thousand acres of Florida tidal marsh were treated with dieldrin pellets that were air-dropped at one pound per acre to destroy sandflies. The fish kill was nearly complete, amounting to about 1,175,000 fishes (20-30 tons) of at least 30 species. Shellfish seemed to be unharmed by dieldrin, but crustaceans were virtually exterminated. Nearly the entire aquatic crab population was destroyed. The larger game and food fishes succumbed most rapidly. Crabs set upon and destroyed the moribund fishes, but next day were dead themselves. Snails continued to devour fish carcasses. After two weeks, no trace remained of the litter of dead fishes.

When Michigan biologists were struggling to augment the new coho fishery of the Great Lakes in the early stages of that historic transplant, they found that three-quarters of their 1967 brood of Lake Michigan cohos were dying from DDT poisoning before the hatchlings got beyond the larval or yolk-sac stage. The same insecticide problem hit lake trout hatcheries in New York State only a few years before. The DDT is accumulated in the yolk-sac that supports the early days of life of the fry and it destroys the newly born fish in less than two weeks.

Ed Joseph of Virginia's Institute of Marine Science thinks DDT may have knocked out the weakfish, a once popular species that virtually disappeared from the coast north of the Chesapeake after World War II. At the time of this writing, the weakfish, however, has been making a miraculous comeback and it is the hope of every angler that this fine food and gamefish does return in great numbers. At the same time, it is interesting to note that the use of hard pesticides is being systematically eliminated in parts of the area.

Another classic case is the near extinction of salmon in New Brunswick's Miramachi River, in the mid-50s, by aerial spraying of the surrounding forests with DDT at one-half pound per acre to kill the spruce budworm.

But biologists are mostly concerned with the deeper effects that are not revealed so willingly. For example, what happens to the eggs of Hudson River striped bass which have been found to contain nine parts per million of DDT and its derivatives, twice the pesticide content that wipes out the Michigan cohos? Yet, this much DDT in eggs is not a total surprise when other tests have shown that stripers accumulate an average of 64 ppm of DDT in their body fats. And have you stopped to wonder where that DDT goes when you eat the striped bass? Don't forget that these pesticides have a cumulative effect and that they do not break down very quickly.

COASTAL PROBLEMS

The 80,000 miles of U.S. coastline are the latest conservation battle zone. Estuaries are the shallow, protected, tidal areas where there is a mixing of salt and fresh water. Tidal rivers, marshes, tideflats, lagoons, bays, and shallow sounds along our coasts are all estuaries. These are the most sheltered parts of the sea for all marine life including fish. Estuaries are also the most fertile lands we have, producing more food than the richest wheat fields in the nation. They are vital to marine life.

Over the years, the estuary regions of the coast have been collapsing as life support systems because of pollution, dredging, construction, bulkheading, and other damages. This has caused depletion of dozens of coastal species, often by wiping out the sanctuaries for the young. In their sanctuaries, the young rely on foods that are totally different from normal adult fare. The food supply of the young is fostered by clean estuarine ecosystems.

The same conditions of pollution that can wreck a lake or river can destroy an estuary. Juvenile fish in their estuarine sanctuaries feed off a food chain that starts with plants and ends with invertebrates. As the juveniles begin to grow, small baitfish are often included in the diet. The young come into the estuaries for two purposes. They must have protection and they must have an adequate food supply in the form of crabs, shrimps, zooplankton, and baitfish.

Whereas pollution is sometimes only a temporary blight on the estuaries, physical disruption does permanent, irreparable damage. Filling operations remove great hunks of the estuaries. Sometimes, developers keep right on going after they have covered the marshes and start filling up the bays, as they did in San Francisco. Thirty-six percent of San Francisco Bay was eliminated by filling before the Bay Area residents became shocked into action in 1963.

Dredging is at its worst when bay bottoms are sucked up and dumped in shallow water or on marshes to "reclaim wetlands." As the bottom is torn out, plant life is destroyed and sediments are loosened to shift about with the current. The silt eventually settles in thick masses on the bottom, suffocating animals and plants in the process. As the adjoining marsh or tideflat is covered with the spoil, everything there is killed and the bay's most essential lifeline is snuffed out. Bulkheads, installed to hold this fill in place, seal the fate of the marsh by blocking tidal flushing which normally cleanses the area and carries the nourishment (bits of plants, etc.) from the marsh to the bay. In the end, the marshes are obliterated, bottoms ravaged, and bays impoverished.

Navigation dredging often adds to the disruption of estuaries. At times and in certain situations, there might be valid reasons for opening a channel or keeping one open. However, the consequences must also be considered. When channels are widened, deepened, or rerouted, sediments are loosened and are carried in suspension. These sediments not only increase the turbidity of the water, but they block out the sunlight needed by phytoplankton and rooted plants to survive. When the silt stirred up by the dredging finally settles, bottom life is buried and will suffocate.

Very often, so-called navigational dredging by independent operators is only strip mining in disguise; their real objective is to mine and sell sand, gravel, or oyster shell. There are many damaged communities along coastal estuaries that were bilked into having a deep channel constructed. The deal was appealing because the cost was so low. But the officials of these towns failed to realize that the dredgers were making huge profits on selling the sand and gravel, while the public inherited an ecological desert.

Much of our productive marshland is a battleground between man and his mortal enemy, the mosquito. Here, war is waged by ditching, leveeing, and poisoning—all of which can inevitably destroy the natural productivity of a coastal marsh. Effective water management programs can reduce the number of mosquitos and still retain the vigor of the marsh in most places by adjusting water levels to prevent these insects from breeding. In the Northeast, these pests can be held entirely in check by providing accessways for killifish to get to all of the mosquito-breeding areas. The killifish devour the larvae.

Highway builders bring further problems. In addition to the disruption of dredging marshes to build causeways through them, engineers often fail to provide for tidal exchange under the roadways. A highway that is built without the benefit of ecological enlightenment becomes virtually a long dam, cutting through marshes and turning the heads of lagoons into stagnant backwaters that soon become polluted eyesores. Any construction along the coast where estuaries are involved must always take tidal action into account. The tide is a flushing agent, and if it can't reach a particular area because of man-made blockages of any description, the adjacent water has to become polluted.

The estuarine environment is brackish—a mixture of fresh and salt water—and when that mixture is correct, that's where the highest productivity occurs. Since fresh water must enter an estuary from a river or lake, it is equally important to recognize that what happens upstream can also have a pronounced effect on the estuary. A dam or a reservoir may cause damage since it impedes the normal flow of fresh water. A dam upstream of an estuary can also prevent anadromous fish such as shad, striped bass, or salmon from reaching their spawning grounds, and it can prevent the downstream migration of the young.

We all want clean water.

And we all want healthy aquatic life. Not simply because we want to catch fish and to know they are free from contamination, but also because we want these underwater creatures and plant life to continue to enjoy their rightful place on this planet.

But the job ahead isn't easy. Conservation groups face a difficult task because their goals require spending tax money and restricting business. If environmental laws are too stringent, business will leave an area. The cloud of unemployment already hangs over some communities. Those who depend on an industry for their livelihood hesitate to interfere with its activities. Private enterprise, by tradition, is the foundation of our economic, political and social system, and public officials and the courts have been reluctant to make decisions that interfere with the system. Nevertheless, some businesses are beginning to share in pollution abatement and control.

These businesses need your support and encouragement. Patronizing those industries that share your concerns and are willing to do something about it, or discriminately buying products designed to minimize or eliminate certain areas of pollution, are a few ways you could help. Giving active support to conservation-minded legislators who have put themselves on the line, is another way. Equally important is simply being vocal about the many threats to our natural resources. Talk to politicians, your neighbors, your friends. Get angry. Write letters.

For if we all intend to continue fishing, we have to do something about it. The 50 million fishermen in this country are a strong minority, but a minority nevertheless. Still, the minorities of this country have been getting things done lately. Maybe it's time for the anglers to express themselves and apply political pressure where needed. Every fisherman has time to spend a few leisure hours each month on conservation activity. It's the only way the job will get done.

12

Fishery Management

Fishery management has been defined as the art and science of producing sustained annual crops of wild fish for recreational and commercial uses. The federal government, every one of the fifty states, and numerous private groups and individuals now practice fishery management to some extent. Simply stated, management of our fishery resources is vital to continued sport fishing in many areas of the country.

MANAGEMENT CATEGORIES

Fishery management can be separated into three broad categories: (1) catch regulation; (2) population manipulation; and (3) environmental management.

Most of us are already familiar with catch regulation, the laws that establish bag limits, size limits, and closed seasons. Somebody decides when the season on a specific species should open, when it should close, the size fish you may keep, and how many of the species you may retain. Usually, the decision is made by a professional fishery manager who takes a number of factors into consideration in arriving at the judgement.

Population manipulation includes stocking lakes and streams, thinning out populations, and otherwise adjusting the various species present. It often involves the creation of a balance between different species in the same body of water.

Finally, environmental management attempts to improve the habitat of fishes through the elimination of pollution, the physical alteration of streams, the fertilization of lakes, and similar water-control activities. Fish ladders around dams or high waterfalls can be considered habitat improvement. Water level adjustment below dams or in reservoirs are another form of habitat improvement.

Fishery management is not an easy task. All three categories of management have their place, and if you talk to enough specialists, you'll discover that each has its devotees. But whether you are talking about catch regulation, population manipulation, or environmental management, you must recognize that each method is limited in its chances for success by how much it conflicts with nature's own plan. And nature leaves little room for man-made miracles.

HISTORY OF FISHERY MANAGEMENT

Fishery management has a history of trial and error experimentation, of fads, of notable successes and spectacular failures. To add to the biological and ecological complexities, management is by nature a political process. Each plan advanced by an agency attracts cheerleaders and detractors as it submits to screening by state legislatures, fish and game commissioners, and angling organizations. But inevitably, bad management programs die and good ones survive. It is not our intention to convey the idea that fishery management is a hit or miss discipline. It is a science and, as in other scientific pursuits, research has led to new and more effective technologies. Funds are sometimes scarce and much needed projects often have to wait, but the men in the field are dedicated and competent.

The early trend in fishery management in the United States was toward increasing restrictions on fishing—that is, catch regulation. It stood to reason that if one were to limit the number of fish caught and the size of the species that could legally be taken, plus providing a closed season to protect the fish population, the stock of fish could be controlled. This practice reached a peak in the mid-thirties and the early forties, but the trend was reversed by the mid-1940s when Tennessee, Ohio, and other states began to experiment with relaxation of regulations for warmwater lakes. To the surprise of many opponents of the policy, fishing improved in most test lakes when closed seasons and size limits were removed and bag limits for many species were relaxed.

At the same time, increasing attention was paid to the environmental aspects of management. Today, with few exceptions, any type of management policy proposed is thoroughly scrutinized in terms of its potential ecological ramifications. In the present period of ecological sophistication, many of the older techniques of catch regulation are still in use. Sometimes these catch regulations are of value and in other situations they are not. Their use today depends on a total management concept that considers all three aspects together. According to Dr. George Bennett, in his book *Management of Lakes and Ponds*, the old restrictive ideas were originally based on concepts of fair play, but doubtful scientific premises.

Bennett lists five early concepts of fishery management. (1) Each angler should have a fair opportunity to take his share of the crop of fish. (This follows the concept of fair play.) (2) Fishes should be allowed to reach maturity and spawn at least once before they are caught. (A false biological concept.) (3) An ample brood stock must be carried over into the following year. (A questionable concept because of the indefinite interpretation of "ample".) (4) Fishes must be allowed to spawn unmolested by man. (This is now believed to be false.) (5) The harvest of fishes must be so unselective as to forestall an overabundance of less desirable species. (Again this presumes fair play.)

It is unfortunate that the early regulations did not
harmonize with the ecological facts of life. Many lakes
became crowded with half-starved runts that died before
they reached legal size because of our ecological ignorance.
Fish are naturally very prolific spawners and the young must
suffer high mortality rates to keep the population in balance.
Nature never intended that all the thousands of eggs laid by
a female largemouth bass in her lifetime should grow up into
thousands of legal-size bass. Nature's plan is that, on the
average, only *two* of these will survive to replace each male
and each female existing in the population. If an average
female were to spawn 25,000 eggs in her life, 24,998 would be
expected to die before reaching adulthood—victims of
starvation, predation, disease, or natural catastrophe. When
we manage fisheries, we substitute a man-made system for
the natural one, and we have to make provisions to
compensate for altering natural controls. One of these
provisions can be to encourage anglers to thin out stocks of
undersized fish so that the remaining ones can prosper and
grow to larger sizes.

CATCH REGULATIONS

Bennett believes that "... angling mortality is probably far
less important in the dynamics of sportfish populations than
most fishermen are led to believe." Scientific studies have
shown that fishermen often catch far fewer fish in warmwater
lakes than those that die of natural causes. Today, bag limits
are often used simply to spread a fixed catch among a greater
number of anglers. But it doesn't always work out that way in
practice, because some anglers are much more skilled than
others. And the skilled angler is the one who usually accounts
for most of the fish.

A detailed three-year study was made on effects of size
limits on trout fishing in the North Branch of Michigan's
Au Sable River by fishery biologists D. Shelter and G.
Alexander. A section of the river was set aside for fly fishing
only, and the minimum size raised from 7 to 9 inches, while
the bag limit was cut from ten to five fish per day. The re-

searchers found that the old 7-inch size and 10-fish limit (any lure) produced better fishing in the long run than the test section with higher size and lower bag limits. The fish spared by the test regulations appeared to die from natural causes during the winter, bringing the population of the special section down to the same level as those sections with normal regulations.

However, in certain situations, catch regulations are often a desirable management tool. The problem with most catch regulations is that they are too rigid. They are applied on a state-wide basis with little regard for specific bodies of water. Every stream and every lake in a state varies from year to year. For example, if a lake should have an unusually successful brood of bass, and the yearlings are so abundant that they may become stunted, or if they are too predaceous on the fry of other species, the manager should be able to suspend size limits and bag limits until balance is achieved. Management can only be effective when the individual manager is granted considerable autonomy so as to be able to make optimal tactical decisions on the basis of existing conditions. Regulations should be free of political influence so that fishery managers can function immediately to correct perceived imbalances.

There is talk among a group of trout fishermen in one eastern state of demonstrating the effects of tactical management to the state officials. The plan calls for managing a portion of one stream independently of the state through a professional manager hired by the group. The goal would be to foster natural propagation in addition to the hatchery-stocked fish and demonstrate that through tactical, on-the-spot management it can be done. But the plan doesn't stop there. These anglers recognize that fishing is a privilege and one that must be paid for by someone. They agree that every angler regardless of financial status is entitled to the same quality fishing as anyone else in the state. But they also reason that if an angler is willing to pay more, he should be able to enjoy better fishing—more fish and larger fish. So, the group of sportsmen propose charging different fees for different stretches of water. The highest fees would be for parts of the stream that were specially stocked with big trout—trout that were much more costly to raise to the above normal size. At the moment, the whole concept is in the talking stage, but it might prove to be a new twist in fishery management at some future date.

BALANCE OF SPECIES

George Bennett, one of the leading authorities on fishery management, claims that most artificial lakes, large and small, are underfished because ". . . hook and line fishing is not intensive or diversified enough to replace the normal system of natural predation." He points out that a high proportion of fish of a species such as largemouth bass are naturally wary and hook-shy. They may freeload all their lives and never be caught by an angler. Therefore, he suggests that unrestricted fishing may be beneficial, including commercial fishing for the removal of coarse fish. Even where commercial fishermen were routinely taking sport species and then were prevented by law from doing this, the fishing did not improve. In fact, the reverse has occurred in places such as Reelfoot Lake, Tennessee (14,500 acres), where abolishment of commercial fishing was linked to a decline in sport catches. In this case, the lake obviously became crowded with undersized, hard-to-catch fish. It doesn't always work out that way, but anglers should be alert to the problems of underfishing and the fact that they can be as serious as overfishing.

At times, managers have deliberately brought in commercial fishermen to cull the rough fish out of a lake. In Morris Reservoir, Tennessee, commercial trammel nets removed 90,000 pounds of rough fish, then 40,000, and finally 13,000 pounds in successive years. Since the commercial catches comprised only 3 percent game species, it appeared that commercial culling could be employed to weed out the rough fish without hurting sport fishing. The authors of this report recommend the netting be done only once every three to five years because the rough species can be so rapidly diminished. There are, of course, many situations where commercial fishing would be detrimental to angling. But the above example indicates that banning commercial fishing is not a stock solution that should be applied across the board. Each lake is a separate system with its own unique characteristics and problems, and should be treated as such.

POPULATION MANIPULATION

In the realm of population manipulation, management is also a complex art-science where pat answers are a scarce commodity and ecology thwarts human ambitions. Much of the manipulation effort is aimed at reaching a balance of species within a body of water where all species are at an optimum abundance. This goal often requires elimination of certain species and filling in with other species raised in hatcheries. The goal, of course, is tailored to provide the best sport fishing. Managers have learned over the years which species can be combined together in any lake or reservoir for the best results.

Again George Bennett did some of the best experimental work on lake management using largemouth bass and bluegills in Ridge Lake, Illinois (18 acres). He started with 435 largemouth bass in 1941 and added 129 bluegills in 1944. From 1944 to 1967 Bennett engaged in a wide series of practical tests, and no further stocking had to be done because the original planting of the two species prospered so well. During that time, 29,700 largemouth bass and 390,000 bluegills were taken from the lake. Bennett's major research method was scheduled drawdowns of the lake from one to three years apart. During the drawdowns, he would cull out any excess of small fishes. He found it necessary to eliminate a high proportion of both species during the drawdowns to achieve best results from the lake. Among the bass, 16,400 fish were culled out, while 13,300 were taken by anglers. Among the bluegills, 337,300 were culled and 52,700 caught. Thus the angling harvest was nearly half of the largemouth, but only one-sixth of the bluegills.

For most lakes, drawdowns are typically planned for fall or

winter, the lake being refilled again in early spring. The lake is often reduced to less than half its normal size during the drawdown. The technique works in several ways to improve fishing. Populations are thinned out because prey and predators are crowded into a much smaller area of water and into unfamiliar territory where there is less protective cover from plant growth. The excess populations of small fish are then far more vulnerable to large predators. Reduced supplies of food for the smaller fish, shortages of oxygen, and other stress factors weaken the unfit or unhealthy fish and increase their vulnerability to predation. The exposure of the bottom around the shallow edge of the lake is also believed to have beneficial effects because accumulated organic matter has a chance to disintegrate through oxidation. Sometimes, crops of millet are planted on the exposed bottom in early-season drawdowns to attract waterfowl for the benefit of hunters. Where drawdown programs work, their efficiency is most welcome because large bodies of water can be manipulated very inexpensively for management purposes.

In Nimrod Lake, Arkansas, a single test drawdown, from 3,600 acres down to 700 acres, resulted in a substantial increase in the populations of largemouth bass and white bass, an amazing increase in water transparency from 1 foot visibility up to 4 feet, and greatly improved fishing. In addition to simply emptying and refilling the lake, 85,000 pounds of commercial species of rough fish were removed.

Drawdowns are also an effective tactic for modifying spawning success. This method is sometimes used for reducing the carp population in a lake. The technique is to drop the water right after the carp have spawned in order to reduce the number of fry that survive. Rapid filling is sometimes used to promote the survival of the fry of game species. As an example, pike fry have a better chance when the water level is raised to cover new spring plant growth over the exposed bottom. The plants, of course, afford maximum protection for the tiny fish in their early stages of development.

STOCKING

Stocking is a major tool for manipulating fish populations. The most common purpose is to create an instant source of catchable-size fish. This is usually referred to as "put and take," in which the stocking agency puts the fish in a specific body of water and sport fishermen catch them. Stocking is also a valuable tool in augmenting or modifying a natural population. Where lake reclamation projects have been completed, stocking is used to replace natural populations. And, of course, stocking can be used to introduce species to newly created bodies of water or in bodies of water that never contained the species before. In most cases, put-and-take stocking appears to have little significant effect on the natural ecosystems or the natural populations in the same waters, because the stocked fish either die or they are removed rapidly. Close accounting showed that 50 percent of the trout stocked in California streams were caught within 3.6 days after release.

Thus, put-and-take stocking has little bearing on normal management programs. Its principle use is in those fisheries that do not lend themselves to sufficient natural propagation or where tremendous numbers of fish are required to meet the demands of anglers.

When a lake or pond becomes heavily populated with undesirable species such as suckers or buffalo, the best solution may be to annihilate all the fish and start over again. This is usually done either by draining the lake dry or by poisoning the fish with a toxicant like rotenone. Often, poisoning is done in conjunction with a partial draining of the lake. After all of the fish have been killed, the basin is refilled and stocked according to the desired mix of predator and prey species.

The stocking of Lake Taneycomo, Missouri, with rainbow trout was done in an effort to replace the warmwater fish populations. This was necessary, according to biologists J. Fry and W. Hanson, because a new dam was built which was to release cold water (40 to 60 degrees F.) from a low level of the new reservoir above Taneycomo. Bottom waters instead of surface waters flowed through the dam. As expected, the warmwater species such as bass and sunfish were virtually wiped out by the cold water, but trout prospered. Four years after erection of the dam, rainbows were making up 99 percent of the catch of 0.6 fish per hour's fishing in the lake.

The most popular stocking combination for years was largemouth bass and bluegills. The bluegills were supposed to forage on invertebrates, become prey for the bass (insuring larger bass), and also afford sport for anglers who enjoyed catching bluegills. The bass, through their predatory activity, were supposed to feed heavily on bluegills and keep the population down, maintaining an overall population balance. What appeared to be an excellent formula in theory didn't always work out in practice. The bluegills often turned the tables on the bass by raiding their nests and eating masses of young bass. The effect was to keep the bass population down while the bluegills flourished. And once the bluegill population got out of hand, there was no way for the bass to reduce it effectively. The bass-bluegill program appears to work better in the southeastern states where the recommended stocking ratio is 30 fingerling bass and 400 bluegills for each acre of lake surface. In fertilized ponds, the ratio of 100 bass to 1,500 bluegills per acre is recommended.

Although the stocking of bass and bluegills is practiced throughout most parts of the United States, it must be recognized that this can only be a short-term program. As explained by George Bennett, "To control bluegills indefinitely, bass need assistance." Bennett found that largemouth will eat crayfish or even their own young in preference to bluegills. He also found that populations of bass by themselves are as large (or larger) in pounds of bass per acre than in lakes where they live in combination with other species of fish.

Stocking setbacks are not confined to only the bass-bluegill formula. Scientific data on walleye stockings in hundreds of lakes and rivers points up that in most instances there is little evidence to indicate that these plantings have been useful. Where walleyes survived, they did not always reproduce—perhaps because of depredations on their young. Yellow perch, minnows, sturgeon, catfish, and suckers all fed on the eggs and larvae of the walleye. Another possible reason for the failures is that the walleyes were put into ecosystems that were already at full carrying capacity and where they could not find a suitable habitat or an unoccupied niche for themselves.

It is quite possible to overstock a body of water. For example, California biologist Norman Reiners reports that the stocking of 1,790 fingerling brook trout was just too much for a 2½-acre mountain lake in California. Growth of the trout virtually ceased after the first year. At the end of six years, the trout had reduced the bottom organisms on which they fed to less than one-sixth of the original abundance.

In any stocking program, fishery managers are hampered by the notoriously poor survival rate of hatchery-raised fish. Hatchery fish are forced to face three basic problems when they are released in the wild. Competition for space with wild fish (native born or already acclimated) of their own species can lead to territorial fights in which the hatchery fish are almost certain to be the losers. Then there is the problem of learning to forage on natural foods after being fed hatchery rations for months. And finally, there is the difficulty in evading predators, because hatchery fish have never had to face one before. A Russian biologist, I. I. Girsa, suggests an ingenious solution to the last problem. He advocates putting a few predators such as pike in the hatchery ponds in order to train the hatchery fish to avoid predators before they come up against them in the wild. Young fish very quickly develop a "predator avoidance reflex," even from just watching another fish being caught and eaten by a predator.

SELECTIVE REMOVAL

Another way to get an ecosystem back in balance is to net out the unwanted species or to try to selectively poison them. Selective poisoning is used to thin out overcrowded stock of desirable species such as bluegills. For example, bluegills are sometimes poisoned out just before the bass spawning period to reduce their predation on bass eggs and young. The gizzard shad, often a nuisance fish, can be killed by light doses of poison without killing gamefishes. But poisoning must always be carried out cautiously and selectively with a full knowledge of the consequences. Rotenone, for example, not only kills fish but destroys zooplankton. This subsequent loss of food will materially reduce the survival chances of gamefish fry and interfere with plankton-eating forage species.

Fishery managers have attempted to zero in on sunfish by locating and poisoning out their nests with poisons such as copper sulfate crystals. However, this tactic is not always successful. For example, intensive poisoning of bluegill nests in four small Michigan lakes produced a reverse effect; that is, it resulted in *more* bluegill fry than in previous seasons. The reason could probably be attributed to lessened competition among the fry. This is typical of the frustrations managers face in trying to improve on nature.

Sometimes a lake is deliberately left with the gap created by selective poisoning to allow the surviving fish to fill it by growing larger. But often an attempt is made to plug the gap with prime species. The species to be stocked must be those that harmonize with management goals and are both biologically and ecologically realistic. Although pike may be a desirable gamefish, they cannot be introduced into a lake with sunfish as prey because pike are poor at cropping sunnies (as are walleye and muskellunge). Muskies are almost always impractical and must be considered a luxury fish. They are costly to raise in hatcheries, they take far too long to grow to trophy size, they eat other fish voraciously, and they don't reproduce well in nature. Cost accounting has shown that a 30-inch muskie in the creel may well cost the state over $200.

Even in the best lakes, muskies are thinly scattered. Diver Ray Hoglund, an expert on muskellunge, once did an underwater census of a Wisconsin lake and found only fifty-eight muskies along a four-mile stretch of the shore. The excitement of musky fishing may well make the cost worthwhile, and some lakefront communities do a thriving business based on this prized gamefish. On the other hand, because of the cost involved, it may be better to go all out for bass instead of muskellunge. Yet, the musky is a prized gamefish and in spite of economics, it would be sad to see it disappear from the scene.

When the dominant population of Ford Lake, Michigan was shifted from yellow perch to bluegills (through poisoning and restocking), the total pounds of fish in the lake increased almost 2½ times. This increase in biomass occurred because bluegill feed lower on the food chain, eating invertebrates instead of fishes. More of a lake's productivity is thus converted into flesh. Higher total production in pounds of fish can be achieved this way, but someone first has to decide if the 2½ pounds of catchable bluegills are more desirable than the 1 pound of catchable perch.

MANAGEMENT MIRACLES

In a few cases, fishery managers have achieved a minor miracle by stocking fish that have been transplanted from far away. By pure luck, the striped bass stocked in San Francisco Bay in the 1800s exploded into a huge population that has supported the Bay Area's major sport fishery for two generations. It all started with two batches of New Jersey bass, taken across the country by rail and introduced into the Bay in 1879 and 1882, a total of 435 fingerlings. Now, Bay Area anglers take millions of stripers per year. Striped bass are now being stocked in a number of freshwater impoundments across the country with the hope and anticipation that they will provide top-rated sport in the years to come.

In a recent trial where ecological design was used rather than pot luck, coho salmon were introduced into Lake Michigan to hold down the populations of alewives—a herring-like, saltwater, plankton-eating fish—that had entered the lake via the St. Lawrence Seaway and had exploded into a huge population of nuisance fish. The cohos caught on like magic and a year and a half after they had been stocked, a fabulous sport fishery developed. This was possible because there was a niche available for them—a great ecological gap caused by the virtual eradication of lake trout by another sea invader, the parasitic lamprey eel.

After the success with the coho, plantings of Chinook salmon (another Pacific species) was started, and it now looks like the Chinook will take hold in the Great Lakes just as the coho did.

But despite the advantages of a systematic ecological approach to transplantation, such a method is not always possible. At times, the job is just too complex for the amount of research funds available. Then, the alternative is trial-and-error stocking of various species of fish. When the Salton Sea became too salty for freshwater fish, California transplanters tried stocking striped bass, corvina, mullet, silver perch, and thirty other species. Out of this mix, two good sport species survived—the orange-mouthed corvina and the silver perch. As a result, there is now good fishing in the Salton Sea, particularly for silver perch. Of course, the results might have been even better with a systematic ecological approach.

To the uninformed, it begins to sound like there's not much to transplanting fish from one area to another. Yet, it is a dangerous practice that requires extensive knowledge of the subject and detailed study of the area. With the successes achieved by the planting of cohos and Chinooks in the Great Lakes and the introduction of species such as the striped bass in several freshwater impoundments, more and more sportsmen are calling for the introduction of non-native fish to their region. If we look back into the history of transplants, however, we will easily discover that there are more disasters than successes when the trial-and-error method is employed. Carp brought to North America from Europe have ruined many good fishing waters by crowding out other species and roiling up the bottom in whatever lake they occupy. That doesn't mean that the carp is totally worthless; many anglers do enjoy carp fishing. But since the majority of fishermen shun the carp, this species not only fails to provide the sport intended but prevents the coexistence of other, more desirable species.

Rainbow trout introduced into the Great Smoky Mountains early in the century displaced brook trout and then provided poor fishing themselves. Brown trout brought in from Europe have been known to displace brookies, rainbows, cutthroats, and Dolly Vardens. Bass placed in trout waters have often displaced the trout.

LIMITS OF MANIPULATION

Experience shows that one can alter the species mix or the sizes of fish in a natural lake, but the total carrying capacity usually cannot be increased by population manipulation. To give you an idea of the carrying capacity by species in lakes and reservoirs, we include the following table (originally reported by biologist K. Carlander):

SPECIES	POUNDS PER ACRE	
	Minimum	*Maximum*
Trout	4	40
Walleye	7	30
Pike	9	22
Yellow perch	9	30
Largemouth bass	13	60
Channel catfish	15	60
Crappie	25	70
Bluegill	40	150
Carp	100	500
Gizzard shad	175	450

Unfortunately, the least desirable fish can be supported in far greater abundance than the sport fishes, with the ratio often exceeding 10 pounds to 1. This difference in carrying capacity occurs because the gamest fish are the top predators.

ENVIRONMENTAL MANAGEMENT

At present, environmental management is probably the most fertile field for converting license fees and tax money into pounds of fish caught by anglers. The goal is to increase the basic productivity of aquatic ecosystems under conditions that insure the maximum yield of desirable sizes. Management of the environment is the ecological part of a total management scheme that also includes harvest control and stocking activities. The first step, of course, is the establishment of goals, and these may be set by the manager or through political process, the customary method at the moment.

The objective of most environmental management is to establish an interacting, balanced community of fish species, each of which will naturally reproduce, feed, and grow with a minimum of assistance. Reproduction will expand the population of each species, while competition, predation, and disease are forces working toward shrinkage. While each of these internal factors must be considered in a dynamic management system, attention must also be given to the external factors such as water supply, predation by birds and mammals, and pollution.

FERTILIZATION

There have been some successful attempts at artificially fertilizing ponds and lakes to increase plant productivity, which, when carried up through the consumers, foragers, and predators of the food chain should result in a higher yield of the gamefishes. H. S. Swingle and E. V. Smith, who experimented with the fertilization of ponds in Alabama, report that they were able to increase the standing crop of bluegills more than threefold—from 130 pounds per acre to between 300 and 500 pounds per acre. For Alabama ponds, Swingle recommends 8 to 14 treatments per year of super phosphate at 40 pounds per acre. The phosphate produces a heavy bloom of planktonic algae that furnishes basic food and also prevents sunlight from reaching the bottom where troublesome filamentous algae grows. In practical application, state biologists I. B. Byrd and J. Crance found that the production of 20 state-owned lakes in Alabama that had been fertilized averaged 129 pounds of bluegills per acre per year and 29 pounds of largemouth bass per acre.

Researchers in many northern states have tried with little success to duplicate the production induced by fertilization in the South. George Bennett's view is that the fertilization of ponds and lakes cannot be recommended as a general fish management technique outside of the southeastern United States, because the results are too variable and uncertain.

Nevertheless Canadian researcher M. W. Smith was able to improve the yield of brook trout in Crecy Lake, New Brunswick, by fertilization and predation control after attempts to achieve similar success by stocking alone had failed. The fertilizer (a combination of commercial types) was broadcast in dry form around the shallow edge of the lake where it produced a plankton bloom. When the plankton used up the fertilizer and died, it sank, thereby enriching the bottom. This, in turn, produced a good crop of bottom life to serve as food for young trout that were stocked. However, Smith found the effect of the fertilizer was only temporary and the nutrients added were eventually lost to the system rather than being recycled by decomposers (bacteria) back to producers (plants).

Other researchers have found the same effect; that is, the fertilizer is used up and lost to the system instead of remaining in the production cycle. Certainly the volumes of nutrients locked up in plankton are lost when lakes are drained in regular drawdown programs. This loss occurs automatically as a result of the natural drainage from a lake, and for balance it must be replaced by the nutrients that leach out of the soil and are carried into the lake by rain runoff and stream flow.

Very often, the need is the opposite. Lakes and waterways become overfertilized and nuisance plants choke up the ecosystem. Heavy growth of algae interferes with fish and with the fishermen. Often the algae dies in masses and fouls the water. Organic pollution (sewage disposal, cesspool leakage, packing house wastes, etc.) is the usual cause of plant overgrowth. To eliminate this blight on the water is a very complicated and troublesome problem. Attempts may be made to kill plants with herbicides, or to physically remove them. Another approach is to stock plant-eating fish such as grass carp that consume 40 to 70 percent of their body weight per day in plant food. Bennett states that a dozen 1- or 2-pound grass carp per acre will control normal plant growth. In the final analysis, an aquatic ecosystem is a delicate balance and must be maintained as such.

Environmental management often involves physical alteration of fish habitat. Streams may be "fixed" to remove obstructions, to provide better flow patterns, or to create better resting pools. New spawning beds for salmon or trout may be created by depositing gravel in strategic locations or old beds that are silted-in may be cleaned up.

ARTIFICIAL REEFS

In salt water there is little opportunity for environmental management because the ecosystems are usually too large and complex, often crossing state lines in the process. Many of the problems are coastal in nature, but there is an effort underway to protect our estuaries—a vital link in the production of many gamefish species. Saltwater problems also involve international fishing agreements, and these must be approached on a federal basis. So, of necessity, most of the habitat improvement has centered around the construction of artificial reefs. The typical setting for a reef is in coastal waters of a depth ranging from 30 to 80 feet, and many have been successful. A wide variety of materials, including junk cars, sunken ship hulls, concrete, rocks, used tires, and old appliances, are being used to build artificial reefs. At the same time, by sinking these worthless items, they are removed from the landscape solving a perennial disposal problem. Placed in a proper location on the ocean floor, such materials acquire a growth of attached marine life—barnacles, sponges, and seaweed. Baitfish are attracted to the reefs to feed on the attached growth and to find hiding places. They are followed by larger predators that feed on them. Thus, a whole community of fish life builds up in an otherwise deserted spot, and fishermen, knowing exactly where the reefs are located, can fish them and try to take the predators.

New fish communities have been started by creating artificial reefs from sunken ship-hulls, old cars, and other man-made junk. The reefs acquire a growth of barnacles, sponges, and seaweed, and attract baitfish and their predators.

South Carolina has been busily building reefs along her coastline out of clusters of old tires cabled to steel hulls, which are taken out to the desired spot and sunk. Once in place, this module is then surrounded with more tires in clusters of three to eight each, with concrete ballast to hold them in place. The reefs are close enough to shore so that anglers in outboard-powered skiffs can easily run out to fish them for spadefish, seabass, triggerfish, cobia, sheepshead, flounder, hake, bluefish, and mackerel.

The Alabama offshore area is flat, sandy, and a virtual underwater desert. A small artificial reef, created when someone dumped a 6-foot-diameter sea buoy and a 15-foot piece of 4-foot-diameter pipe, was discovered by Alabama fishermen in

1962. The reef, located in 56 feet of water, was fished that first day by 21 boats, and the fishermen said that they had to stop fishing early for fear of sinking their light craft with a heavy load of red snapper. One charter boat with seven anglers aboard fished for only one hour and boated 1,500 pounds of red snapper.

Off St. Petersburg Beach, Florida, tire reefs yield good catches of cobia, grouper, sheepshead, mangrove snapper, speckled seatrout, and Spanish and king mackerel. Off New York and New Jersey, the tire reefs yield seabass, blackfish, whiting, cod, and porgy in season. Artificial reefs are springing up in more and more places along the coastlines of the United States.

Artificial cover is also being used in fresh water, particularly in many of the northern lakes. Most of it is dragged out on the ice during the winter and allowed to remain. As the temperatures warm in early spring and the ice melts, the car bodies, cribs, trees, and other debris break through the ice and sink to the bottom. This cover can be particularly valuable in providing more habitat for gamefish, and many of the projects are undertaken by local fishing clubs.

THE FUTURE

As human population increases, and as industrial activity intensifies around the country, fishery management becomes an increasingly complex and difficult occupation. George Bennett's opinion is "... that one would be naive to expect any combination of fishes, stocked or native, in a natural or artificial lake to be productive of good fishing for an indefinite period of time. Too many of the integrated forces and counterforces that were active for promoting the well-being of a fish population in a primitive environment are absent from today's man-dominated waters."

Fishery management is not a new science, but its progress has suffered over the years from a continuous lack of funds. National and local priorities usually place fishery research way down on the list, and it is for that reason that more is not known about the underwater environment. However, it is clear that the key to good fishing in the future rests with the professional fishery manager and the willingness of the fishing public to respect and abide by his decisions. There's no doubt that trying to outdo nature is a delicate and serious business. Mistakes can be extremely costly, and the results of errors in judgment can be with us for a long time. The story of the introduction of the carp in the United States is a good case in point.

On the other hand, there have been great success stories, such as the transplant of the coho salmon in the Great Lakes. Yet, the truly difficult work of the fishery manager is on a day-to-day basis, trying to manipulate populations, establish catch regulations, and improve the habitat. Many of these projects can be undertaken by local sportsmen's clubs, and it might be worthwhile to check with your local fishery manager to find out what you and your friends can do to help. The end result will be better fishing for everyone.

Photo Credits

Index

Index